6/13

The Coming Draft

The
Coming Draft

The Crisis in Our Military and Why Selective Service Is Wrong for America

Philip Gold

Ballantine Books
New York

Published in the United States by Presidio Press,
an imprint of The Random House Publishing Group,
a division of Random House, Inc., New York.

PRESIDIO PRESS and colophon are trademarks of Random House, Inc.

ISBN-10 0-89141-895-4
ISBN-13 978-0-89141-895-5

Printed in the United States of America on acid-free paper

www.presidiopress.com

9 8 7 6 5 4 3 2 1

FIRST EDITION

Design by Mary A. Wirth

To my wife
To my son
And to their generations

Contents

"In war, one does all kinds of jobs."
"Then I'll wait for the declaration of war."

ALBERT CAMUS, L'Hôte

"John went on to serve his obligation honorably.
I weaseled out honorably (and never regretted it)."

YALE ALUMNUS, CLASS OF 1970, reminiscing in
Yale 70 by the Class of 70, 35th Reunion, 2005

Acknowledgments

CLEMENCEAU ONCE SAID that war is a series of catastrophes leading to victory. Anyone who has ever written a book, knows that process.

This book went through one of the worst catastrophes that any work in progress can face: the question *Does it matter anymore?* In fact, this book went through it three times.

I first conceived *The Coming Draft* in 2004, as the Iraq war's appetite for American lives and money began to engorge, and as rumors of a postelection draft swirled about. Having written one prior book and over twenty articles on conscription, I wanted to do what I could to impale this particular blood-sucking vampire. By the time my agent, Stephen Barbara, sold the book, draft rumors were OBE and the youth of America and their "influencers" (Pentagonese for family, friends, role models, and significant others) could return to their regularly scheduled anxieties.

Still, I had a book to write. I pondered and procrastinated, wondering why it still mattered. Then the second crisis. In the fall of 2005, it became apparent to anyone even mildly attuned to Beltway defense antics that the Pentagon had given up on the American people. They'd decided that they couldn't attract enough good young men and women to serve and, anyway, they'd rather spend the money on things. For a few weeks, I toyed with changing the title to *Expendable*, a study of how the Pentagon now planned to work its present force to exhaustion and beyond, perhaps hoping they wouldn't have to. These folks really don't want to do any more Iraqs. Meanwhile, my editor, Ron Doering, was waiting for a book. Time also flies when you're not having fun.

Does it still matter? made its final appearance on the morning of Friday, January 26, 2006. For weeks, it had been clear that the Defense Department intended to cut people. Meanwhile, America's attention was sticking like Velcro to James *"A Million Little Pieces"* Frey's megabucks inability to distinguish fact from fiction from fantasy, and his tawdry, tacky, betrayal of Oprah, who had first exonerated him on the grounds that the message mattered more than the truth. (Were these two planning to go into politics together?) Then I learned that the QDR, the *Quadrennial Defense Review*, due out in February 2006, took as its theme "The Long War," positing at least twenty more years of strife.

My first thought: Twenty more years and they're cutting forces? Who wrote that document, James Frey? Hamas had just won its first Palestinian election and was already talking about establishing a Palestinian army. The Iraq war, which I opposed from before the beginning, was shambling along toward whatever awaited it. And the neocons were gurgling about how we gotta hit Iran next, and while we're at it, let's destabilize Syria.

My second thought: *The Coming Draft* now matters far more than when I started. It matters because, in effect, the Defense Department has decided that only a catastrophe can really get this people's attention, a catastrophe that would induce the federal government's standard spasmodic response to disaster: spend money.

But this time, also, draft people.

The book got finished only a few weeks late. Ron was more gracious than he should have been. We offer *The Coming Draft* as a warning that, unless we get serious about what we're doing in this world, and why, and how, *A Million Little Pieces* may soon describe our national defense. I happily acknowledge Stephen and Ron and their fine work in making this book possible. Many of the military people I've spoken with must remain anonymous, for personal and professional reasons. I would, however, like to acknowledge three excellent, invitation-only military list-serves and discussion groups I'm privileged to access: MILINET and Webmaster Anthony; the Warlord Loop and the Warlord Himself. And the members of these groups are savvy; listening in has taught me a lot. Thanks also to the good folks at "G-Two Forward."

Thanks also to Admiral Bill Center, USN (Ret.), and to John M. Titcomb.

Thanks finally to my son, Jonathan, who turned eighteen during the 2004 draft scare. He told me that he had no military interests or ambitions. When I asked him what he would do if conscription were reinstated, he replied that he would stay out of the Army the same way I did, and join the Marines.

Semper Fi, son. Semper Fi.

MERCER ISLAND AND SHELTON, WASHINGTON
July 2005 to June 2006

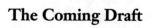

The Coming Draft

Introduction

IN THE SPRING OF 1981, a mere eight years after starting, I finished my Ph.D. Elation was tempered by exhaustion, relief by the fact that I was finally abandoning my semiperpetual student lifestyle for that sad but unarguably adult status: unemployment. My degree was in history. Tenure-track jobs back then were about as common as horse eggs. White males of conservative *tendance* need not bother to apply.

My prospects, however, were not excessively fatal. My dissertation was on advertising. I'd done a stint in business school and had become enamored of marketing, a hormonal rush of an endeavor, combining rigorous methodology with exuberant chicane. Madison Avenue was an option, even if martinis made my head rotate and pop, and cocaine was anathema. More hopefully, I'd been developing my freelance writing market and was becoming known among the senior neocons. Perhaps something might come of it.

Something came of it. One evening I found a letter in my mailbox, return address but no name on the envelope. I was about to trash it, but the stationery seemed too upscale for junk. I opened it to find a letter from the Smith Richardson Foundation, inviting me to apply for a grant. Fatigue forgotten. Elation again. Modern U.S. cultural history was my passion, especially the issues that had coalesced into Culture War I, that 1960s to 1990s thirty-year tantrum I'd been living as well as studying (we're into Culture War II now, but that's a subject for another time). I'd been a conservative, an uneasy, not-quite-True-Believer conservative, since Goldwater '64.[1] I'd sensed that the movement had a dangerously limited and far too hostile view of America's social and cultural defects and travails and needs, and could use a more enlightened perspective. Now Smith Richardson would fund me to provide it. I would pay off my library fines, collect my diploma, and write the study that would knock their intellectual socks off.

I put my proposal together and invited myself to New York to discuss it. I sat before the program officer, Mac Owens, and explained everything. He paused a moment, then rubbed his face with one hand in a universal gesture of skepticism and said:

"What we're really looking for is someone to do a book on why we need the draft back."

My crest not only fell, it hit the floor with an audible thud. The last time I'd considered the issue of conscription was my senior year in college, 1970, when my draft notice arrived. I was furious, and not just because I was legitimately IV-F, medically unqualified, by reason of asthma, hay fever, and a few other maladies with ominously multisyllabic names that always seemed to be prefaced by the word "nonspecific." I was certainly getting an allergic reaction to my government's latest communication. *How dare they* tell me that I *had* to do something? I got out my finest remaining stationery and scribbled something on the order of:

Dear Draft Board,
    Thank you for sending me this induction notice, which I am returning to you. I have no intention of serving in the United

States Army. I will never serve in the United States Army. Please
stop wasting my time, your time, and the government's postage.

Sincerely yours.
Philip Gold

P.S. I recently joined the Marines.

Eleven years later, I found myself briefly wishing I hadn't, or
that I'd taken my battery gunny's advice and stayed in ("Lieutenant,
you'll never be this happy again"). Sitting there, hopes for cultural
impact evanescing, I gave my program officer—a former Marine
with a Silver Star and two Purple Hearts from Vietnam—to understand that I could be far more valuable as a Culture Warrior operating behind radical lines, conducting raids on "psychologized ethics,"
and rescuing issues such as women's rights from the feminista. He
countered that a Jewish Marine with my fancy degrees (B.A. Yale,
Ph.D. Georgetown) was ideal to take on the draft issue. No, they
didn't expect an imminent return to the draft, or even a serious political movement in that direction. But it mattered to keep the issue
alive, against the day when conscription would be possible again.

The phrase "Semper Fi" is never to be confused with the
Marines' motto *Semper Fidelis*. "Always Faithful" states an inviolable
creed, while "Semper Fi" can have several dozen different meanings, depending on situation and tone of voice. So when I gave Mac
Owens the obligatory "Semper Fi," he understood.

It wasn't what I wanted. But fifty thousand to write a book and a
year as a senior fellow in a no doubt prestigious think tank held a
certain appeal. And so began what turned out to be a twenty-five-
year ponderization of two of the strangest ideas that human beings
have ever come up with.

First, that a democratic state has the right to tear its citizens
from their homes, families, and private endeavors in order to send
them anywhere the government desires to suffer, fight, kill, and die.

And second, that the citizens of a democratic state have the right
to refuse.

A few months later, embedded in a suitably right-wing think tank in the section of Washington, D.C., later to be known as Gucci Gulch, I settled down to write what became my first book, *Evasions: The American Way of Military Service*. It wasn't a bad first book. It was certainly sensitive to the funder's desires, to conservatism's predilections, and to the general tone of the Reagan years. But it also left me uneasy. Despite (or perhaps because of) all the research, my opinion of conscription hadn't changed, nor has it since. To put it into a vocabulary accessible to politicians, policy analysts, media "opinion leaders," civilian "influencers," and every young person in America: Conscription sucks so bad, you get hickeys on your brain just thinking about it.

But military service . . . that was different. Always, I'd clung to the antediluvian belief that every American male should spend some time in uniform as a normal part of life and of citizenship. I still do—viscerally, at any rate. I never saw much sense in Vietnam. By 1970, few people did. Four years on an Ivy League campus, however, had convinced me that the opponents of the war, and the outlooks and vocabularies and self-justifications they were so zestfully manufacturing, might ultimately harm the country more than the war itself. I chose to take a stand or, as the deed was also known, to make a statement. Conscientious objection was personally and politically abhorrent. (It still is, although, were the draft to resume, I would extend the right to everybody, no questions asked. More on that later.) So was cashing in on my medical deficiency.

It proved easy enough to do a dodge. I simply forgot to mention fifteen years of schnorks and sniffles and sneezes and sprays and shots, just check off *no* at the relevant places on the medical history form. Back then, they operated on the principle that if there was anything wrong with you, you'd flaunt it; they didn't need to look. I then chose the Marines, who, I suspect against their better judgment, chose me. Acceptance did nothing to improve my then-fiancée's mood, Vassar girls not being noted for their martial enthusiasms. Mine, however, when I asked her if she was crying because I joined

the Marines, replied with Vassar-like candor: "No. I'm crying because you wanted to." My soon-to-be father-in-law, a prosperous
dentist with a profound dislike for hippies, radicals, and "Moratori-
umniks," plus an odd affinity for Spiro Agnew and an absolute lust
for Richard Nixon, also got candid. After expending considerable
energy on dissuasion, he suggested that, if I had to serve, I should let
myself be drafted and he would make up the difference between officer and enlisted pay. When I asked why he would do that, he
replied, "It would be easier to explain to our friends."

Semper Fi, Dad.

Officer Candidate School, that intricately structured and inti-
mately supervised initial transition from Ivy League intellectual to
lieutenant of Marines, was endured. Then TBS, The Basic School,
where the Marines send their neonate brown bars for training. (It's
abbreviated "TBS" because the standard acronymic usage, "BS,"
was deemed an inappropriate commentary on the curriculum.) The
Marines were pulling out of Vietnam; a training accident that left
me in a leg cast for six months precluded a tour. Three-and-out, or
so I thought. I did my three, then entered grad school. Two years of
academic inanity later, with the Vassar girl and I gone our separate
ways, I got to missing the Corps. A colonel of my acquaintance
guided me into the abysmally mislabeled Organized Reserve. Since
I had some MOSs (military occupational specialties) that were in
short supply in the active Corps, and since I could usually get away
for a few weeks . . . let's just say that one reason the damn dissertation took so long was that I could usually get away for a few weeks.
By 1981, I was a major. I had loved it. But the time had come to slip
away from all things military and do my cultural gig.

It never happened—at least not full-time. I spent the next two
decades plus as, variously, a think tank defense analyst, journalist
covering defense, author, and college professor teaching "war and
society" and other defense-related courses. Whenever the subject of
conscription arose, I was more than happy to note that it wasn't
needed, it wasn't wanted, and that whenever we'd practiced it, the

results had always been unjust, uneven, and unsatisfactory. "Bad faith" was the phrase I used more than once to describe America's experience with the draft.

Then came Iraq.

Although I supported the Afghan invasion and the Bush doctrine of preemption and regime change in the abstract, from the spring of 2002, I opposed the Iraq venture and the whole notion of turning the *Umma* into a neocon theme park. My opposition was based on the fact that I could count, and knew that we would run out of pearls—military, monetary, moral, metaphysical—long before the world ran out of swine. I also sensed the likely answer to a question nobody cared to discuss during the run-up to hostilities. "After Saddam, what?" I did not believe that the United States should be trundling around the world, forcing people to be free, or mortgage our future to the secular redemption of the Middle East. In sum, I suspected that this would be a significant failure of that endlessly venerated and oft-invoked but rarely practiced conservative prudence, the art of applying general principles to specific situations. My public opposition (plus other matters) led, late in 2002, to my departure from a conservative think tank where I'd been senior fellow in national security affairs, ending a ten-year affiliation. It was, by the standards of think tank terminations, amicable. It was time to go. I went.

Then came the ugly aftermath of "Mission Accomplished" and, starting in 2004, calls for and speculation concerning possible resumption of the draft. I now found myself opposed to conscription for another, more personal reason: a son in high school. A strong and wonderful young man, smallest starting offensive lineman in his school's football league, plus lacrosse on a state championship team. Like so many of his contemporaries, he's patriotic in a quiet, nononsense kind of way. And like so many of his peers, he doesn't quite connect with the military. His sophomore year, the Marine recruiters paid his high school a visit. Since Mercer Island is an affluent community, they didn't waste a lot of time there. Jonathan approached one sergeant and mentioned that his father had been a Marine. The recruiter blew him off with a "Come back and see us senior year." So riled was I when he told me, I called in a formal complaint, then went out to the Officer Selection Office (different folks) to pick up some literature. An hour later, the gunnery sergeant in charge politely kicked me out. It had been decades since I'd spoken with a real live gunny, and my ardor finally wore out his patience.

Nothing came of my trip. Midway through his senior year, I began to understand why. His advanced placement government teacher had assigned Chris Hedges's *War Is a Force That Gives Us Meaning*. I asked him why, if this was true, he and his friends weren't lining up outside the recruiter's door. He smiled and replied, "We have more sense."

That stance, respectful of the military but unimpressed by the uses to which it has been put, motivated me to write this book, and to do it right. But what, exactly, is right? Anyone taking on this subject, especially anyone who wishes to produce more than a rant or a screed or a "Here's your money, here are your conclusions, go write the book" monograph so beloved of the policy gerbils and their funders, quickly discovers three facts.

First, the published and Internet literature on conscription is humongous, while the related literature (history, philosophy, political theory, public policy, sociology, personal memoirs, websites, etc.) is several orders of magnitude humongouser. Much of it might be described as repetitive, redundant, and repetitious, but a lot of it, even the more derivative stuff, seems pretty good. At best, you pick and choose, usually with a sense that, even though you know what the "canonical" works are, you're probably missing the best, or at least the most interesting, pieces. And so I should like to offer a preemptive apology to those whose good works I may have overlooked, or whose good works were simply unavailable. I also apologize to the descendants and admirers, if any, of General Enoch Crowder, who ran the World War I draft and whose memoir, *The*

Spirit of Selective Service, I was absolutely unable to locate on library shelves, interlibrary loan, Amazon, or eBay.

The second fact flows from the first. It's hard to avoid the impression that everything's been said. The arguments for and against conscription, or national service with military and non-military "options," have been around for centuries. You can pick up books and articles from 1916 or 1940 or 1969 or 1990 and have a pretty fair fit with today. Situations and enemies may vary, but the underlying philosophies and perspectives do not.

And from the first two facts flows the third. Nothing has been said precisely because everything has been said. Put differently: In modern America, public discourse is usually less than the sum of its parts. Far less. We're informed to stupefaction, and misinformed and disinformed and counterdisinformed, yet also oddly and sometimes invincibly ignorant. Tell me once or twice, I get it. Tell me three times, I'm sure. Tell me a hundred times and MEGO (mine eyes glaze over). Far too often, debate consists, endlessly, of people hurling prerecorded messages, prerecorded long ago, at and past one another. From those in power (I hesitate to use the word "leaders"), it's mostly lies and spin and talking points and vague, high-sounding generalities. And denials. If you want to know what's really happening, track the denials. That, or tune in to Comedy Central.

Meanwhile, from the allegedly serious media, its sound bites and trivia and "If it bleeds, it leads" and the noxious debasement of turning everything into entertainment and (the American Way) turning entertainment into porn. Why, more and more, do the anchors and pundits—of both genders—seem like TV wrestlers, playing their hokey, bombastic characters? Why so much junk? Because we want it? An old Madison Avenue adage holds that some of the people making the commercials are fully as stupid as the people they think they're talking to. The insight is apt and too often applicable outside that profession. And who among us would care to wear a T-shirt proclaiming "Proud Consumer of Garbage"?

But when we try to speak to one another as citizens, seriously, in words of reason and meaning and with respect . . . how often does that happen anymore? Can it even happen anymore? There's a pornography of insult abroad in this land. Yes, the Founding Fathers, A. Lincoln, and F. D. Roosevelt were not strangers to that sort of thing. But they and their generations had something more. Do we? Or perhaps it might be more appropriate to ask, Can we get it back?

We can. We are not—despite the best efforts of our media and educational conglomerates, and despite the strong desire of the Republocrat imperium that we remain oblivious and docile—either a stupid or a passive people. We just need to get our bearings back. We need to regain the art of talking to one another. Let the politicians and the officials continue to address us in words carefully chosen to convey no meaning. Let them get huffy and snippy and hissy, as they're doing more and more, whenever they're seriously questioned. Let's take a break and just talk with one another. Don't worry. The Beltway and the media will still be there when we're done.

Which brings me to Aretéa and my desire that we speak to one another as citizens on a matter of extreme national, indeed planetary importance.

Some years back, I'd played with founding my own think tank. Aretéa—the name derives from the Greek *aretē*, meaning "virtue" and "excellence"—foundered on funding. Grant-makers know what they seek and rarely subsidize that which strays. "Tell us what we want to hear, the way we want to hear it" is not an epistemology confined to consumers of Fox News or hard-left websites such as Not in Our Name (which I track on the Net and very nearly ordered their Cindy Sheehan wall calendar last Christmas). Penniless and boardless, Aretéa gradually morphed into an informal writers group, consisting mostly of people who were dissatisfied with the quality of thinking and discourse in their respective fields. Members include physicians, journalists, lawyers, defense analysts, two fine young marine Iraq vets with books out, and a self-taught stone mason/philosopher. Gradually, we developed (please pardon the pomposity) an "Aretéan" approach. To address any public issue, do three things:

Break the debate
Assess ideas and solutions without regard to their origin
Talk to people like they were people

"Breaking the debate" means getting beyond the preformatted arguments, the symbiotic posturing, and the mutual sneers. This may be done by finding a new approach, offering a new perspective, or simply asking the reader to "zeroize" his or her mind—forget everything you know, at least for a while. If you can't do that, then consider adopting a principle I took to heart as a Marine Corps intelligence officer.

It's OK to be 70 percent certain that you're 100 percent right. It's OK to be 100 percent certain that you're 70 percent right. But if you're 100 percent certain that you're 100 percent right, you're either wrong or you're going to be.

"Breaking the debate" works. For example, Discovery Institute, the think tank from which I parted over Iraq, has done a brilliant job of popularizing "Intelligent Design" as an alternative to the either/ or of evolution vs. Biblical creationism—at least until they took it to court and got their buns handed to them by a Bush-appointed federal judge. One of our Aretéans, a retired radiologist turned journalist, argues that the real crisis in medicine is neither money nor lack of insurance per se. It's a dozen different but cumulating "refusals to treat," from individual physicians giving up and getting out to HMO and government rationing. The approach gets people listening, often skeptically, but that's all to the good. Take nothing on faith. Get your brain going. Think.

Second, seek and scavenge and scrounge for insights. Not exactly "If your enemy has a good idea, steal it." From the Aretéan perspective, there are few enemies, save those convinced of their own infallibility and those violent extremists who hold that your desire to live and your enemy's desire to kill you is a difference of opinion. The point is to get beyond the fetters of category. Consistency may or may not be the hobgoblin of small minds, but categories such as "liberal" and "conservative" and "bipartisan" certainly constrict the flow to the brain. If breaking the debate entails constructive uncertainty, the quest for ideas is based upon the notion that sometimes freedom begins when you say *No!* to those who tell you what your choices are. Get over it. Get beyond it.

Finally—and this is crucial—speak to people engagingly, and with respect. Both aspects matter. Engage them. Respect them. The primary audience here is the citizenry of the United States. Those who are serious and those who want to be. One type of citizen in particular. There is in economics a concept of "rational ignorance." People are busy. Issues are many and complex. It makes no sense to waste time and effort comprehending matters that have no relevance to your own life, or upon which you have no hope of acting and impacting. There is, however, a kind of citizen who values broad understanding and is willing to devote perhaps a few hours to some subject. That's the person to reach. But to do so, you must offer something more than the standard bilge, hype, spin, or oatmeal. If someone is going to take the time to read your book, then give value for value received. Far too much of what passes for information and debate nowadays neither requires nor rewards serious attention. Make your reader work.

This book, then, is an offering to the citizens of the United States that requires and hopes to reward serious attention. It deals with life and death. It presumes no prior knowledge of conscription, its history and prospects, or of related and ancillary matters: defense policy, constitutional law, the Just War heritage, ethics, demography, whatever. The gist of these matters will be provided, based upon serious scholarship and analysis. However, this is neither a scholarly nor a policy tome. It is academically informed but not academic; policy-oriented but not policy-driven. It notes, but does not get involved in, the feuds and fussages of various political and policy factions. There's a D.C. adage: "Where you sit determines where you stand." That doesn't always make you wrong. It does mean that you oversell, overcriticize, and, in the latter stages of intellectual sclerosis, adopt "I can't disprove it, I just don't like it, so I guess I'll get mad" as your rhetorical strategy.

This book seeks, then, to avoid immersion in the disputations of the interested parties, and of the experts, both men and women, who sometimes seem to have spent their professional lives addressing one another and talking mostly about themselves. It also minimizes the roles of the oft-invoked and too oft overanalyzed "usual suspect" thinkers of the past. We can do this very nicely with only a nod or two toward Locke and Hobbes. We can also elide anyone who has ever written or will ever write on Just War theory (a checklist of categories you can manipulate to justify any conclusion you want), John Rawls, and whatever Thomas Jefferson did or did not opine on any given morning, afternoon, or evening. I'm also declaring this book an Alexis de Tocqueville Free Zone.

That felt good.

Finally, this book suggests that, as they said back in the sixties, "The issue is not The Issue." The subject under consideration is, narrowly, the draft; more broadly, military service. But broadest of all is the question: Is there, can there be, any morally compelling, rationally structured, and militarily effective relationship between service and citizenship in the world and the age now upon us?

The Issue, though, is what to do in and about the world and the age now upon us. Does any of this really matter anymore? And that's why, before going any further, we're going to "break the debate" on this matter. We shall do this by defining, at least provisionally, the nature of the world and the age now upon us, and suggest that issues of conscription and service, although currently atop nobody's list of concerns, will matter again greatly. And sooner than anyone thinks.

· · ·

WHEN THE COLD War ended, the United States found itself, for the first time in seventy years, without an imminent threat or even a serious enemy. Nor did any "peer competitor" seem likely to emerge for decades. So tranquil did the world now appear that Francis Fukuyama, a hitherto obscure think tank denizen, rose to full national intellectual status on one article, proclaiming "The End of History?"[2] According to Dr. Fukuyama, the Big Questions had been solved. All that remained was to service the machinery of the victors, that triumphant tandem of liberal democracy and welfare state capitalism, and to extend their benefits to the 80 percent of the planet who hadn't quite dragged their boats to the appropriate shoreline, where they could be lifted by the rising tide. And we were all, predicted Dr. Fukuyama, going to be very bored.

There are some mistakes so ridiculous, only experts can make them. Even if Dr. Fukuyama did append a question mark to his title, his opinion was clear, and has taken its place in intellectual history alongside Bernard Brodie's 1946 assertion that while once the job of the military was to win wars, now its job was to prevent them. Other experts, however, and other men and women in power, were making less amusing mistakes, based upon their own notions of reality and their own visions for the twenty-first century. One group, the liberal "Muscular Humanitarians," happily endorsed the then-regnant cliché that "The [Russian] bear may be gone, but the woods are still full of snakes." America might not be going forth in search of dragons to slay, what with the present and foreseeable dragon shortage, but snake-hunting was an acceptable second-best. It was, in fact, more than acceptable, provided we did it with sufficient gusto, if not always sufficient fortitude. This we did, in places like Somalia, Bosnia, Kosovo, and a few other locales, sadly not including Rwanda. The effort was expensive. Results were mixed. We were not always thanked, or even welcomed. Still, at least according to the Clintonista, it was fitting and proper, at long last, to be using our forces for humanitarian interventions and peace-keeping, not war—least of all those old-fashioned wars of neocolonial oppression masquerading as high-virtue anticommunism. So satisfying was this vision of the American future to liberals that from time to time I would suggest that the next beneficiary of our armed humanitarianism should be Samovia. Save the Samovars. More than a few agreed with me, at least until they punched up "Samovars" on Google and got referred to eBay.

A third post–Cold War vision was far less benign. The "America's Greatness" crowd, centered on the younger generation of neocons, began casting about for a career-long crisis worthy of what they deemed to be their talents. Their demands for a new National Purpose—"America without greatness isn't America; let's go thump somebody"—saturated their journals and sluiced onto the op-ed pages of the "prestige," now sometimes called the "legacy," media. Open letters to presidents were written (especially about Iraq), faxes blasted, heads set to talking on TV. But these were the Clinton years of peace and prosperity and a good cup of Starbucks coffee every time. And who knew from Osama bin Laden when Monica Lewinsky could be tittered over and upon?

Nine-eleven changed all that. Or so it seemed. President Bush took up proclaiming that, whether Osama was brought to justice or justice brought to Osama, justice would be served. He also told America, "Go shopping." Whatever needed to be done, would be done quickly and well, without any of the messiness attendant upon rousing this people to war, or asking it for sacrifice, or for hate.

But that, as they say, was then. This is post-then. Nearly five years into the struggle, we still don't even know what to call it, let alone how to win it. The government and the chattering classes have tried to market their crusade without even sussing up a decent brand name. Can't call it a crusade: culturally insensitive. So sometimes it's WOT, the War on Terror. Sometimes it's GWOT, the Global War on Terror. For one brief nonshining moment in 2005, it was

GSAVE, the Global Struggle Against Violent Extremism. A few among the right-wing punditry, less AO (acronym obsessed), package it as the war on Islamo-fascism. Others opt for World War III, World War IV, Fourth Generation Warfare, Fifth Generation Warfare. And then, of course, there's that peculiarly neocon entry, "Hard Wilsonianism"—making the world safe for democracy, this time with the "will" (along with "nerve," another neocon fave) to make it stick.

Nothing has stuck. Perhaps "The Long War" will, but even that tells us less than we need to know. And for over a decade now, the Kennan Prize, the nonexistent yet highly coveted award that will go to the person who explains the twenty-first century the way George Kennan nailed the Cold War, remains unclaimed. The following may not win the Kennan Prize. But it offers a glimpse into a possible future and suggests why the question of citizen military service, conscripted and/or volunteer, may prove far more vital to our future than anyone has yet been willing to recognize, or dare to admit.

Please try this on as a possible way of viewing the twenty-first century, a prelude to our consideration of whether the citizens of the United States need fight for their country, or anything else, anymore.

> The age of the Wars of Ideology is over. The age of the Wars of the Ways has begun. And over the next couple of decades, these new wars may well segue into the greatest crisis humanity has ever known.

The Wars of Ideology lasted a tad over two centuries, 1770s to 1990s, more or less. They began with Lexington and Concord, ran through the democratic revolutions of the nineteenth century and the cataclysmic struggles of the twentieth. They ended with the rendering of the Berlin Wall into souvenirs, soon enough to be available on eBay, and with Boris Yeltsin standing atop a tank in Moscow's Red Square, facing down the last of the Soviet Union's

alcoholic apparatchiks. Like the Wars of Religion of the sixteenth
and seventeenth centuries, the Wars of Ideology were about more,
far more, than their names indicate. But clearly, the Wars of Ideology entailed two great collective questions. What is the proper form
of political organization? And what is the proper form of economic
organization? Dr. Fukuyama was far from entirely wrong. These
great questions had indeed been answered. Some form of liberal
democracy, coupled with some form of market economy, does more
good for more people than anything else yet devised. So compelling
was this victory, so common the assumption that freedom was indeed the wave of the future, that you could almost hear the fundamental questions of the new era being posed.

If the Wars of Ideology were about collective matters, now we
would focus on more individual concerns. Specifically: What does it
mean to be human, and more fully human? Politics and economics
would now be placed in the service of human rights and human welfare. War would be regulated accordingly.

This is no exaggeration. Consider our own domestic concerns.
Questions regarding the nature and extent of human existence and
rights now dominate American political life, from abortion and capital punishment to immigration to what went on in Abu Ghraib.
They affect, powerfully, attitudes and practices toward globalization, toward the conduct of war and the nature of peace, toward
whom we succor and whom we sanction. We desire not just a kinder,
gentler world but a more fully human one. And this desire is, I am
persuaded, both proper and sincere. I opposed the Iraq venture because I considered it politically imprudent and militarily wasteful,
the wrong war in the wrong place at the wrong time against the
wrong enemy. But we are right to adopt as our national purpose a
kind of guardianship of the twenty-first century, moving the human
race toward a more perfect habitation of its own existence, according to our abilities and opportunities.

Unfortunately, as the old military adage avows, there's always
some son of a bitch who doesn't get the word. Or in the present in-

stance, a few billion souls who either aren't interested in a kinder, gentler world or who are but who can't seem to find their way in.

Today, the condition of the world is mixed. There are a few hopeful signs. The rate of global population increase is falling, even though regional overpopulation and mass migration remain severe concerns. Incomes are rising here and there, thanks at least in part to globalization. The most absolutely destitute now appear slightly better off. Democracy, what Churchill called the worst form of government except for all the others, seems to be taking hold in parts of Latin America and Asia, maybe even China someday. Of course, democracy doesn't always produce results congenial to American policy makers. (When Woodrow Wilson fumed in 1913, "I will teach the South American republics to elect good men!" he only had to worry about Hispanic, not Islamic, elections.) Perhaps Iraq will stagger into something decent, after all. And although the number of armed conflicts around the planet remains surprisingly constant, usually in the sixties, deaths are trending down—at least when measured from a Cold War baseline. It might seem that if we could just deal with those nasty terrorists or insurrectionists or rejectionists or Islamo-fascists or whatever you choose to call them, Dr. Fukuyama could claim the Kennan Prize after all. And we could all go shopping without that dim, uneasy sense that there's more bad stuff out there, and it's headed our way.

We can't. We won't. Osama bin Laden is part of something far larger and far more pernicious than a few thousand (or million?) crazies who fantasize about toppling the United States and restoring the caliphate. He and his successors are part of a growing web of movements and forces with very different agendas but a single common objective: to escape from the freedoms and possibilities, the greater *human-ness*, of the twenty-first century. Violent Islamic extremists. Racial and ethnic separatists. Ecoterrorists. Old-fashioned political criminals and kleptocrats. Leftover Marxists and Maoists. Organized transnational crime, in league with local gangs and rapaciously recruiting in our hideously overpopulated prisons and among the millions here illegally. Those who can't abide twenty-first-century culture and mores. And the gurus and gauleiters of philosophies and movements yet to be imagined.

The Wars of the Ways, then, will pit those peoples, nations, and regions that partake of the twenty-first century, its freedoms and possibilities, against those who want out. Those who want out will have and use weapons of mass destruction (nukes and enhanced conventional explosives), weapons of mass death (chem/bio), and weapons of mass disruption (EMP, cyberwar). And those who want out will be allied with those who can't get in: the three billion of us who live on less than two dollars a day, amid conditions of anarchy and squalor (whether in Africa or in France), and who embrace as their working philosophy, "When you got nothing, you got nothing to lose."

It's happening now. It will go on. Afghanistan and Iraq are only the opening campaigns of a very long struggle. And we're going to get hit again. And again. And again.

Now factor in ecological deterioration and global climate change and its potentially catastrophic effects. We have already lost our first city, even if the government and the official chattering classes don't care to label it as such. The weather is now political. Now factor in the possibility of deadly new germs and pandemics. Now factor in American debt, the endless accretion of obligation at all levels, public and private, and the certainty—yes, the certainty—that the increase cannot be sustained forever without consequence. Now factor in the unknown and unknowable consequences of new technologies, especially the probable union of genetic engineering and nanotechnologies. Now factor in anything else that you care to list, from asteroids to Armageddon, and you're in the realm of the *Titanic*.

The *Titanic* did not become synonymous with disaster just because it hit an iceberg. A confluence of events and omissions made disaster inevitable. If only the ship had been designed a bit differently. If only the bridge crew hadn't forgotten their binoculars. If only that ship ten miles away had kept her radio on. If only they'd carried enough lifeboats for all.

If only. If only. If only.

It is possible to imagine a twenty-first century beset by strife. Only the dead, said Plato correctly, have seen the last of war; humanity has seen over 6,500 recorded wars these last five millennia, plus everything else that went on. But it is also possible to conceive of a world ever more promising and humane. And it is also possible to envision a confluence of human and natural forces that will present this species with an absolute challenge to its existence.

America cannot win the Wars of the Ways militarily, and should not try. We will win by doing everything in our power to get those three billion souls into the twenty-first century while dealing rationally with the impacts of natural disasters and changes. But America can lose the Wars of the Ways militarily. We can fail to win the battles that must be fought in the shadows. We can fail to manage the fact that maybe half the countries on this planet have borders that don't make political, social, cultural, economic, or ecological sense, and that some divorces—amicable or nasty—are in order and may be inevitable. We can squander our forces on peripheral threats, such as Iraq. And perhaps most important, we can fail to reengage the people in the common defense, which is, in the end, the common defense of this planet. We must reconnect citizenship with service, in a manner morally, politically, and militarily consistent with this new set of challenges. This book aims to restore the connection between citizenship and military service, in a way that is right for the era and consistent with our deepest values, a way that speaks beyond the issue itself, and to us all as citizens.

Mise-en-scène

THE WARS OF THE WAYS are the struggle of those who accept and partake of and defend the twenty-first century—its freedoms, diversities, and possibilities—against those who (to borrow from Milton) would rather reign in Hell than serve in Heaven, or at least decline to participate in a world striving for a greater fullness of life for all. Those who want out of the twenty-first century will often—not always, but often enough—be allied with those desperate billions who can't get in, or haven't yet gotten in. Far too much disputative energy has been expended on whether or not terrorists are poor or middle class, ignorant or educated. Suffice it to say that the Internet-fueled Revolution of Rising Expectations—How you gonna keep 'em down on the farm (or in the madrassa) after they've seen enough *Baywatch*?—no longer permits the desperate billions to believe that everybody lives, or has to live, the way they do. F. Scott Fitzgerald once wrote, famously, that the rich are not like you and me. Ernest Hemingway retorted, yeah, they have more money. In the twenty-first century, the greater the world's expectations, the less the awe, or the need to respect those who have what so much of the world still lacks.

They'll be weak, our enemies, preposterously weak by the standards of conventional force. But thanks to weapons of mass destruction, death, and disruption, they'll be able to do heinous damage from time to time, or perhaps practice blackmail and extortion on an unprecedented scale. They'll also have the aid of nation-states, rogue and otherwise. They may even capture or create a nation or two of their own. It's going to be a long struggle, fought perhaps amid accelerating natural catastrophes. Maybe, just maybe, this century will bring the greatest crisis humanity has ever faced, one that may compel, in Shakespeare's apt phrasing, a simple choice.

Up together to Heaven or down together to Hell.

Maybe. I've been writing and speaking on this way of looking at things since 9/11.[1] No one has ever completely agreed with me, or wanted to. No one has ever liked it. But no one has ever disproved it, or been able to dismiss it. In many ways, I hope I'm wrong. But we'll keep this paradigm, provisionally, in order to assess one aspect of the military dimension of the struggle: the responsibility (if any) of the American citizenry to participate.

To do so, it's necessary to evaluate four separate but nonetheless related matters.

First, what is the status of America's defenses as we head into the post-Iraq/post-Katrina world? In a word, grim. Far more grim than anyone cares to admit. We're rapidly approaching a condition perhaps best described as "defenseless on a trillion dollars a year." Current defense planning and public debate on national security affairs might charitably be characterized as "Franz Kafka argues with Alice in Wonderland while the Three Stooges sit on the judges' panel and the forces of Sauron gather outside the room." A bit less hyperbolically: No nation, no empire in history has ever faced such a complex set of challenges. And perhaps the greatest challenge will turn out to be people. Things can be built and money spent, however inefficiently or pointlessly. But getting people to participate . . . in the end, that's far less a matter of money than of a clear understanding of what's at stake, generating a new civic virtue. Not "patriotism." This is but an emotion that may lead in many directions and rarely requires action. Civic virtue does.

Second, the draft: Is it needed? The answer is not only no, but hell no and no way no how, and we can speak a lot more plainly if you like. Any return to *direct federal* conscription, which is what is commonly called "The Draft," would be both militarily wrong and morally abhorrent. In order to see why, history helps. For the history of conscription in the United States reveals century upon century of corruption, bad faith, and absolutely astonishing inefficiency. This says nothing about the honorable service, accomplishments, courage, and sacrifice of tens of millions of draftees. Nor does it suggest that when opposing the massed armies of totalitarianism, conscription was not necessary. It was. But it was always a difficult, inequitable way to do business, and is neither necessary nor desirable now.

Third, a brace of vexatious questions. If not conscription—and if not pure voluntarism—what? The answer depends on more than military needs, as these are presently defined by the MICE: the military-industrial-congressional empire that spends the trillions we send them in our taxes, plus what we borrow from the Chinese. The answer requires an explicit return to the Founding Fathers' original understanding of both the nature of threats and the relationship of the citizenry to those threats. To the Founders, as to much of the world today, the common defense is a continuum, with individual and local self-defense at one end, proceeding to domestic strife and foreign attack, with overseas federal war at the far end. This was one reason why the Founders cherished the militia and the citizen-soldier ideal; they could operate across the entire spectrum of peril. But they would not operate without constraint and restraint. The Founders' vision was that, while the citizenry held an unalienable

obligation *and right* to bear arms in the common defense, this did
not constitute a blank check on the citizenry by the federal government. Only the United States among democracies has ever assumed
that conscripts could be sent anywhere to do anything. After World
War II, most Western democracies drafted. Conscription was acceptable because the peoples of those nations knew that the service
of their young men and, in the Israeli case, women was limited by
law or custom or both. Switzerland could draft, and still does, because everybody knows that Switzerland isn't about to invade anybody. Great Britain used conscripts in its colonies, but ended its
"National Service" in 1960. After the Algerian war and de Gaulle's
withdrawal from the North Atlantic Treaty Organization (NATO),
French conscripts remained at home. By law, West German draftees
could not be sent outside Germany. When small nations such as
Denmark sent draftees to sit on the NATO/Warsaw Pact border for
a few months, it was clearly understood that they were there for one
reason only: to deter a Soviet attack. For Israel, the 1981 Lebanon
War, also called Operation Peace for Galilee, Israel's first war of
choice, shattered the popular sanctity of Zahal, the Israel Defense
Force. It has never recovered from that mistaken adventure, nor
from the experiences of nearly forty years' occupation duty on the
West Bank.

Vietnam shattered the nexus between citizenship and conscription. And now, Iraq has shattered the nexus between the citizen-
soldier and citizenship. For it is equally wrong to presume that
National Guard members and service reservists can, short of some
overwhelming national emergency, be sent anywhere to do anything
in wars of choice and policy, not of survival.

But there's a matter even deeper than reaffirming the Founders'
vision of defense and the role of the citizenry. Is it possible even to
speak of an engaged, responsible citizenry at all anymore? In recent
years, restoration of such a citizenry has been a major agenda item
for political scientists, philosophers, sociologists, and pundits of
various persuasions. Many have focused on restoring a sense of

"community" and togetherness and a new "sense of sacrifice." The literature on this subject has proven as inane as it is vast, and often camouflages little more than a plea for liberal social engineering, sometimes coupled with national service, with military and non-military options—another hideously bad idea. (Just imagine a federal teenager-herding bureaucracy trying to slot between two and four million kids a year into everything from the Army infantry to changing diapers on infants.) A minority of writers have concentrated on restoring a sense of autonomous citizen "obligation," if only as a partial antidote to the Me Me Me/Rights Rights Rights mentality. This literature can be quite thoughtful. But you will search it in vain for references to any military aspect of citizen obligation. It just ain't there. Meanwhile, another school of political theory and philosophy attempts to tie obligation to "consent"—the kind of consent derived from the fact of membership in a society and acceptance of its benefits and protections. But again, save for a few hard-right writers, you won't find military service reaffirmed, or even much considered, anymore. You will find, however, spirited defenses of the citizen's right to refuse, coupled with that lame, evasive platitude that "dissent" is somehow a higher form of patriotism and virtue than participation.

Still, as I pondered the larger issue of citizenship, I came to the strange realization that objection, not consent, provides the key to justifying twenty-first-century military service, and that no militarily effective system that does not understand objection, legally and culturally, as vital parts of the Founders' vision, can work. This means, among other things, junking the common, and the legal, understanding of conscientious objection as it emerged from the Vietnam War.

The final matter under consideration: making it work. The United States can reengage its citizenry in the common defense. There is a way. But before getting into the details, it's necessary to consider in some detail the three items already listed: the present mess, the sordid history of conscription, and how and why the

Founders have, once again, turned out to be such incredibly smart people. Not just because they read a lot. Not just because they understood human nature. Not just because they could translate theory into reality and use reality to correct theory. Not just because they lived it.

The Founders were smart because they talked to one another about all these things. They spoke in words of meaning, sent between men and women capable of and desirous of reason. Thomas Jefferson (he is hard to avoid) once wrote of the joy of "persuading and being persuaded." Whatever their specific goals and visions and animosities, these people were open to one another in ways we've lost, and need desperately to reacquire. Yes, there was venom back then, and histrionics, and screed. Yes, there was ugly self-interest and even uglier oppression. But they got beyond it because they wanted more, for themselves and their posterity. Their ability to connect with one another, in mutual faith and reason, sustained them in that hard, elusive quest for an ever more perfect Union. It has sustained their successors. Enough of them, at any rate, to permit us to reach this day.

Looking back, history has decreed their victories inevitable. Of course, they were inevitable—to everybody but the men and women who had to go do it. And if they could speak to us now, perhaps they would remind us that neither God nor act of Congress nor presidential order nor Supreme Court decision, nor even the cumulated tonnage of our opinion surveys, has ever decreed the United States of America immortal. It would be a shame to blow it now.

1

The Crisis that Isn't . . . or Is It?

ON OCTOBER 21, 2005, the *Washington Post* ran a letter from Francis J. Harvey, secretary of the army. Most likely, Secretary Harvey didn't write the letter himself. That task probably fell to some junior colonel who may have cringed a bit, but who knew that the official line must be maintained. For its part, the *Post* obliged, headlining the letter: "No Recruitment Crisis for the Army."[1]

"On October 11," the letter began, "the Defense Department released its recruiting figures for fiscal 2005. Much attention has been given to the [active] Army missing its goal of 80,000 recruits by 6,600. Despite some alarmist rhetoric, the Army is not in a recruiting crisis or considering a draft.

"To put this year's shortfall in perspective," the letter went on, "the total of 73,400 people recruited is within 2 percent of the average recruitment each year for the past 10 years." The letter then noted that the Army had exceeded its retention goals, "enabling it to just about make up for the recruiting shortfall." Further, the Army is reorganizing to put more soldiers into combat units. These and other changes "are producing a bigger war-fighting force that is more lethal, more agile, more expeditionary and more efficient."

Concluded Secretary Harvey:

"Recruiting isn't just a challenge for the Army; it's a challenge for the nation. We need young people to continue to answer the call to duty, just as they have during the Army's 230 years of service to the nation."

Two months later, the *Washington Times* reported on an informal effort by a retired general to get the word out: "The Army Isn't Broken."[2] In a letter to the Army community, especially its retired senior members, General Gordon Sullivan, a former chief of staff, now president of the Association of the United States Army, affirmed:

"To suggest to our troops in harm's way [that] their Army is broken strikes me as telling those on the firebase . . . they are not going to do well. Unfortunately, the American public takes the statement at face value. . . . [T]he Army is stretched as well as overcommitted, but there is no evidence to support an institutional breakdown. . . . I think it is remarkable . . . that the leaders and soldiers of the Army have performed as magnificently as they have given the nature of the conflict."

Urged General Sullivan: "The Army is not broken. Talk with our troops and their families."

Once again, you learn what's going on by listening to the denials. And once again, invocations of soldierly virtue and accomplishment attempt, ineptly, to veil bureaucratic and institutional failure. I asked a retired Army colonel, a three-war combat veteran who went on to a distinguished second career as a civilian analyst, if he thought the service was broken. "No," he responded, "but it's bent." He might as well have answered, "No, but it's pretzeled." Twisted half a dozen different ways and, in the manner of pretzels, brittle. Very, very brittle.

I also paid attention, via a couple of invitation-only military list-serves I'm privileged to access, to the comments of a variety of active and retired Army officers during the period between these two letters. The pattern was clear. Denial, usually accompanied by anger that such a thing could even be suggested, then invocations of their own experiences and harsh words against those who dared insult the troops—criticism always "insults the troops"—by suggesting there might be a problem. It was unpatriotic, a dissing of America, a giving of aid and comfort to the enemy to acknowledge:

That recruiting shortfalls in war cannot be put into perspective by comparison to recruiting successes ten years ago, during peace.

That the major combat components of nine out of ten active Army divisions are either in Iraq and Afghanistan, gearing up to go, or recovering from their last tour.

That tens of thousands of soldiers are now facing their second deployments, while at least one Marine unit—First Battalion, Fifth Marines—has returned for its third. Others will follow.

That the Army is now taking men up to 40 years of age, and is offering enlistment bonuses of up to $40,000 plus additional cash if enlistees agree to go into certain Iraq-bound units after they complete training.

That the National Guard and Army Reserve are effectively drained, given the legal limitations on deploying Guard members and reservists involuntarily outside the United States for more than two years in any five-year period without a declaration of war.

That the Army National Guard wanted 63,000 new recruits in fiscal 2005, but signed up only 50,000—after falling 7,000 short in fiscal 2004 and 7,800 short in fiscal 2003—and is currently 17,000 below its (inadequate) authorized strength of 350,000.[3] More recent reports that recruitment is strong, do not yet constitute either a trend or a solution.

That the nation's reserve service components consist of a set of categories, of which two are currently relevant. Some people belong to organized or "selected" units that drill one weekend a month and two weeks in the summer; these are the units that have, since 9/11, been worked to exhaustion. A second category consists of the Individual Ready Reserve, or IRR. This contains people with prior active-duty or reserve service, who have a remaining contractual obligation. They are not affiliated with paid drilling units, but may belong to unpaid volunteer units or be mobilized for training or duty as individuals. Skill levels vary tremendously, from members just released from active or reserve service to those who aren't much more than names in a database.

That when the Army attempted for sixteen months to mobilize members of the IRR, so many failed to show up, or could not even be located, that it canceled the effort. As of December 2005, only 3,954 members out of more than 5,700 call-ups had shown, out of a pool of 115,000. Some no-show officers were permitted to resign, while a few dozen officers and enlisted face discharge boards. Some IRR members are, at least according to rumor, claiming that they never showed because their mobilization notices looked like junk mail, and were tossed.[4] It might be added that, over the last few decades, the IRR has rarely had valid addresses and phone numbers for more than half its roster.

That according to the Pentagon's own statistics, through March 2006 well over 1.1 million men and women (over 143,000 women, to be precise) have served in Iraq, Afghanistan, and at sea in the theater—nearly half the total active and reserve force for one small war in a country the size of California.[5]

That this war is going to go on, with others, like Iraq or not, to follow, and that this force is wearing out.

But there is no crisis, we're told, only misguided and/or malevolent people who suggest that there might be one. And in truth, the Army and the Defense Department have decided what to do about this crisis that officially isn't. They have decided to do *nothing*. They have, de facto, given up on recruiting a force adequate in quality and quantity, until such time as a national catastrophe, or a national change of mood, either fills the recruiting offices or mandates a draft.

To say again: Between October and December 2005, the U.S. Army and the Department of Defense effectively *gave up* on drawing enough high-quality volunteers from the American people to meet its own doctrinal and real-world requirements. The master plan of the moment is to slow down even the modest active-duty increase planned, from 480,000 soldiers in 2001 to 512,400 in 2009, and to cut the National Guard and Army reserves.

This is not to suggest that the military wants the draft back anytime soon, or expects it to happen. Indeed, it does not, if only because the Army has little institutional desire to occupy any more countries and would rather spend the money preparing for neat, clean, short, and tidy wars like Desert Storm—or a slugfest with China. It is to say that, in the absolutely vital matter of fielding a force that can do a fraction of what it may have to do, they're content to drift along, hoping for the best while awaiting the disaster that may spasm the government into a new draft. And it does mean that, in order to dodge the people issue, the Army is prepared to work its people to exhaustion and beyond. General Peter Schoomaker, the Army's chief of staff, speaks often of how the Army will soon "break this culture of impoverishment" and field a force that is "fully equipped and resourced."[6] He no doubt means it. But in a very real way, the present force has been deemed *expendable*.

Meanwhile, the Navy and the Air Force have problems of their own. If they both routinely exceed their recruiting and retention quotas, that's because, in this time of war, the quotas are shrinking. In fact, they're letting people go, or detailing them to Iraq to support the Army. As of early 2006, the Air Force had 1,500 airmen pulling convoy duty and another thousand working with detainees, training Iraqi forces, whatever.[7] The Navy has thousands in-theater working outside their normal missions; the service has also established its own Naval Expeditionary Combat Command to handle the War on Terror ashore. This outfit, a composite of combat and support capabilities, represents a grab for new missions and the budgets they generate. It also indicates that those missions are available for the taking from an exhausted Army.

So why are the other services overpopulated? Simply put, it's because they're running out of ships to sail and planes to fly. The Navy has about 360,000 people on active duty, but the U.S. fleet currently numbers only 281 ships, the lowest since the 1930s. Worse, the service has virtually no idea what to buy, or how to afford what they want. According to the latest assertions, the Navy might sacrifice a carrier in order to procure a few dozen Littoral Combat Ships, or LCSs, high-tech patrol craft for inshore work. They may have to, since the first next-generation carrier is now expected to cost well over $10 billion. They may also be hoping—a standard Beltway game—that they'll make the offer, but Congress will pony up the money to prevent the cut. Meanwhile, the fate of the next-generation destroyer, the DD(X), remains unclear, while Virginia-class attack submarines cannot be purchased in sufficient quantity to maintain a force of even 50 boats. The Navy hopes to get back above 300 ships, counting coastal LCSs, maybe sometime in the next decade. All that is certain is that restoring the fleet will cost far more tens of billions than originally programmed, and will come in late.[8]

About 281 ships—but 218 active-duty admirals. By some counts, if you throw in all the reserve admirals and retired flag officers recalled to temporary active duty, you have more admirals than ships. Even the Marine Corps, traditionally the leanest of the services, now boasts 81 active generals, including an unprecedented five four-stars. The Corps now numbers about 180,000; the administration wants to cut it to 175,000.

Meanwhile, the Air Force, currently around 352,000 souls, plans to cut 40,000 military and civilian positions over the next six years. The service has no idea how many aircraft, piloted or not, it will be flying then, or what shape they'll be in. As always, the struggle between the fighter and bomber "mafias" for dominance continues. The service has no clear follow-on to its present long-range bombers (B-52, B-1, B-2), although it has been ordered by the Defense Department to field a long-range strike aircraft by 2018, instead of the original date: 2037. Why they would even consider building such a craft—the current B-2 stealth bomber costs, depending on the accounting used, from $800 million to over one billion each—may have less to do with wartime needs than with keeping the flying club going.

As for the white-scarf-and-goggles set, the Air Force now anticipates buying under 200 F-22 fighters, less than half the original expectation. Meanwhile, Pentagon PBD (Program Budget Decision) 720, December 2005, plans to retire half the B-52 bomber force (56 planes), all the F-117 stealth fighters (52 planes), and all the U-2 spy planes (33 aircraft) ahead of schedule to save a few billion. As with the Navy, this reflects Pentagon gamesmanship: threaten massive cuts, then let Congress find the money. But it also reflects the fact that older planes cost ever more to fly and maintain and that, one way or another, the fleet is going to shrink dramatically. Tankers and transports remain in perennial shortage.[9]

Yes, the new aircraft and ships are far more capable, at least according to the technological indices. But not even the best ship or plane can be in two places at once, and their relevance in what is increasingly called "complex irregular warfare" remains less than totally assured. True, we fight with what we have, and usually well. True also, air supremacy must be maintained across the entire spectrum of conflict. But it does get expensive.

So unless some super-secret new aircraft or pilotless platform comes along that doesn't cost more than its predecessors, the Air Force may drop to less than 2,000 craft. The Air Force does, however, have 273 generals.[10] It also had, effective December 2005, a new mission statement, to "Deliver Sovereign Options for the defense of the United States of America, and its global interests—in Air, Space, and Cyberspace." Nobody's quite sure what that means.[11]

Still, it appears to be a worthy companion to their recent recruiting slogan, "No One Comes Close" . . . catchier, perhaps, than "An Army of One," but maybe not all that appropriate for a service that specializes in precision bombing.

Air and naval shrinkage aside, the fundamental people problem belongs to the Army and its 304 active-duty generals: How can it maintain a 490,000-person force that, in reality, ought to be several hundred thousand larger?

By the by, the ratio of general and flag officers to troops and ships has long been taken as a sign of military health: the more top-heavy the brass, the worse-off the service. Take for example: On December 5, 2005, the Defense Department announced that a retired four-star Army general, Montgomery Meigs, had been named "to spearhead an expanded DoD program to counter the threat of improvised explosive devices," aka roadside bombs, in Iraq and elsewhere. The JIEDD-TF, or Joint Improvised Explosive Device Defeat Task Force, first established in October 2003, has "resources in excess of $1 billion" and will soon establish a "center of excellence" training center.[12] Less than a month later, the JIEDD-TF, still led by General Meigs, was upgraded to the Joint IED Defeat Organization (JIEDDO) to add, according to *Inside the Army*, "permanent organizational structure." "The office will also stand up a 'distributed' Joint Center of Excellence comprised of the combat training centers of the various services. . . . The center of excellence 'will develop operational techniques and tactical procedures, and provide a venue for the integration, training, experimentation, and testing of new IED Defeat equipment and concepts,'" a memo from Deputy Defense Secretary Gordon England states.[13]

(The Manhattan Project, which produced the atomic bomb during World War II, turned out its product faster, and required only a two-star to run it. And, to paraphrase a line from a famous movie, it didn't need no stinking "center of excellence." But we digress.)

When in April 2006, I checked on the progress of the Joint IED Defeat Organization, I learned that by the end of 2006, they will have spent over $5 billion on the problem, studying everything from devices that can sniff the air for explosives to satellites. The Army may also ask Congress for $167 million for an alternative approach: building new, purely military roads.[14]

People are the Army's problem; only the Army's needs and deficiencies drive any draft. However, before looking at the present disarray in more detail, it might be useful, or at least humorous, to review the Army's personnel problem in the generic.

To put it bluntly, the wonder is that, personnel-wise, anything good ever happens at all.

In general, twenty-first-century military recruitment faces four problems in attracting civilians, four additional problems in personnel management, one historical fact of life regarding American military planning, and one catastrophe aborning.

Attracting Young (and Sometimes Not-So-Young) Civilians

So why is it that the "interested, qualified and available" pool of young persons is today such a small percentage of America's military-age population? Begin by noting that the military is an intensely old-fashioned hierarchical entity in a civilization that neither values nor practices old-fashioned hierarchy much anymore. The Army (I base this assertion on thirty-five years of observation, plus a significant quantity of Marine bias) remains the most ponderously, morosely, ineptly hierarchical of the services. Indeed, Nigel Aylwin-Foster, a British brigadier general who served in Iraq with the U.S. Army, describes that service as: "imbued with an unparalleled sense of patriotism, duty, passion, commitment and determination" yet is "weighed down by bureaucracy" and "a stiflingly hierarchical outlook."[15]

The Navy may be neurotically hierarchical, vestigium of those centuries when the ship's captain was God and officers dined on starched linen tablecloths, attended by dutiful Filipino stewards. The Marine relationship to hierarchy may be described, albeit somewhat charitably, as manic-depressive. (There are those who must be obeyed, but we're family in ways the other services are not.) We're also quirky. As for the Air Force, the only hierarchy that matters is who flies and who doesn't, a condition that will either intensify or disintegrate as the service runs out of planes.

An additional problem of hierarchy in all the services is promotion by seniority and the up-or-out system. Not everybody wants to wait twenty years to know if they even have a chance of making it to the top.

The second problem after hierarchy is that military life is hard. It doesn't pay particularly well, especially when the economy is benign and civilian jobs plentiful. Even when it's not, you can still make more money as an entry-level burger flipper than a first-enlistment warrior. Living conditions are austere. Boredom abounds. Family separations can be devastating. The work can get you killed.

This leads to the third generic problem. The martial virtues aren't much in fashion anymore. In contemporary America, violence is not something you do on behalf of your country, earning thereby the admiration of your countrymen. In the abstract, maybe. But nowadays, violence (the more graphic the better) is entertainment. Video games and Hollywood special effects are fun. However, people who deal in up-close and deadly contact with real enemies, and who come back from doing it for real, are not entertaining. Granted, societies have always had fears about reintegrating their warriors, sometimes with reason. Often, they've been ignored, detested, despised, then forgotten. Today, however, America has chosen to celebrate its service people in the denatured abstract, fastidiously honoring the dead, paying rote homage to the pain of the wounded and shattered, but offering scant regard for the rendering of violence unto the enemy. We're just not comfortable with that kind of thing anymore. Victims, yes; heroes, no. And not since the World War II generation has a cohort of returning warriors been accorded political and cultural power commensurate with what they sacrificed to learn what they know about the world and its evils.

Finally, while patriotism may or may not be the last refuge of a scoundrel, in modern America, it's fundamentally an emotion that doesn't really obligate anyone to do anything. After 9/11, there was no spike in enlistments. Since the Iraq war began, quantity and quality have fallen steadily everywhere—from Army boot camps to ROTC and service academy applications. In one way, this need not surprise. For three years, the Bush administration has conducted the Iraq war Vietnam-style, without attempting to engage the passions of the American people, or asking for any kind of sacrifice whatsoever. We've offered none, nor demanded to be asked, nor even taken that much interest in the war, one way or another. Some might claim that the nation's utter nonresponse reflects mere apathy and why won't it just please go away? In another, it's the sense that we're simultaneously too big to fail, and even if we do, what of it? Whatever happens in the Sunni Triangle, our malls will still be there. Or perhaps it would be more evocative to suggest that support for this war was at best three thousand miles wide and three inches deep. It's certainly true that the American people never demanded this war, no more than they demanded Vietnam. Perhaps, as in Vietnam, the American people extended the benefit of the doubt to a president who was determined to take the country into war, and did.

But the benefit of the doubt ends when it's your life, or your husband's or your wife's or your lover's or your child's, on the line. Certainly, it takes nothing away from those who serve to suggest that the American people have passed a quiet judgment on this war by our clear disinclination to have at it.

Four obvious problems then: hierarchy, harshness, aversion to the martial virtues, and the nonbinding nature of patriotism, especially at the present time. That's the view from the outside, the view of young people and their parents and other "influencers" looking into the military world. Now to the personnel problems of that world.

Managing Military Personnel

Four additional dilemmas combine here to make military personnel planning and management an exercise in perpetual frustration.

First, the military is one of only two large institutions, the other being the Church, that cannot go outside its own ranks for middle and senior management and leadership. With very few and mostly technical exceptions, everybody starts at the bottom. Your privates today will be your sergeants ten years from now; your lieutenants today will be your colonels in twenty, your generals in thirty.

That is, the selection will be made from those who remain, who are not seduced by the civilian world and its comforts and securities; who love the service but get out in exhaustion or disgust; or who are killed, or who are invalided out.

In the military personnel system, what you start with determines what you end with.

Second, the military has no way of knowing how many people it may need, or what mix of skills it may require, ten or twenty or even five years from now. I once heard Herman Kahn, godfather of the modern think tank, discourse on why the military can't be run like a business. Imagine that the Defense Department is a business that does most of its work during special "sale days" that occur only every decade or two. The business has no idea when those sale days will be, nor who will be the customers, nor what merchandise might be required. They find out only on the morning of the sale, when the competition walks onto the premises, shoots the staff, and starts busting up the inventory. After that, the best this business can do is forget the master plan and improvise. If you guessed wrong ten years ago, too bad.

The third problem: human quality. The old adage "Any mother's son will do" no longer avails. Nor does the recruiter's private slogan, "Customer only has to buy the product once." Poor recruiting years mean poor cohorts working their way through the system, and this is not simply a matter of lousy scores on the aptitude tests or prior acquaintance with the juvenile justice system. Individuals often enter the military to straighten themselves out, to be challenged beyond their previous experiences, or to find new purpose for existence. Many succeed. In no individual case does a mediocre set of initial qualifications automatically preclude later success, even though long experience has shown that decent aptitude test scores and a high school diploma (as a token of self-discipline) are the best indicators of success. The problem lies in a more complex interaction.

As a rule, good people do not join troubled or failing institutions. Those who do often acquire bad habits and may indeed be predisposed to bad habits. In the military context, early experiences are exceptionally formative. Those who entered the Army in 1942 had very different acculturation from those who entered let's say in 1952, 1962, 1972, 1982, 1992, 2002. Their outlooks differ correspondingly. Joining a victorious, or at least a determined-to-prevail army is rather different from joining a force that's imploding due to defeat, exhaustion, or civilian hostility. Two examples, a bit less abstract, may avail.

As the United States expanded its Army for World War II, colonels and generals were in extremely short supply. But many officers who had served honorably and well during the interwar decades were retired or denied field commands. Their peacetime professional lives, and the views and habits acquired therein, had not prepared them for the upcoming campaigns. Thirty years later, as the Vietnam War wound down or, depending on your point of view, spun away, the military began a decade's worth of taking too many people who shouldn't have been there. Mediocre-to-bad people went into a demoralized and impoverished military and behaved accordingly. To this day, few veterans of the 1970s will discuss just what a mess those years really were. Whether this paradigm fits the emerging situation is still unclear. Should the war drag on, or be lost via withdrawal, should the national mood turn antimilitary, the situation might repeat.

Still, it would seem, as Secretary Harvey indicated, that when recruiting turns tough, increased retention can make up for it. But not really. You still have the problem of weak cohorts coming up behind. And too often, under such circumstances, you keep people you'd rather not. The Army does not release detailed retention statistics beyond happygrams proclaiming that it exceeded its quotas again, and occasional reports on which MOSs (military occupational specialties) have been targeted for special inducements. Anecdotal evidence, however, suggests that much of the recent success has been due to a combination of increased bonuses for short-term reenlistments, coupled with fear of "stop-loss," a legal procedure by which service members may be held on active duty involuntarily up to eighteen months after their contracts expire. So how much of the recent quota-smashing was "Hey, buddy, you're gonna be here anyway. Why not take the money?" And even so, according to a GAO (Government Accountability Office) study reported in the *New York Times*, the Army has had great difficulty keeping skilled people. But this is no longer a simple matter of "the airlines or the computer giants are hiring, we're outa here." These are vital combat people, from Special Forces to intel analysts, often lured away by PMCs (professional military corporations) who can offer six-figure salaries. The report, according to the *Times*, concluded that the military "had failed to fully staff 41 percent of its array of combat and noncombat specialties."[16]

And this despite paying out $500 million in reenlistment bonuses during fiscal 2005, four times the annual amount from 2003 to 2004.[17]

What is known—indeed, has been known since conscription ended in 1973—is that the people to be retained in a volunteer, professional force are older, more frequently married, and more likely to have children than a bunch of nineteen-year-olds. The average age in the military is now over twenty-eight. Over half of all military personnel are married; collectively, they have nearly 1.25 million kids, more than 500,000 under age five. And although basic salaries are low, the average service member receives over $112,000 in pay and benefits, accounting for nearly 25 percent of the defense budget, or over $109 billion.[18]

Indeed, this reliance on retention is changing the composition of the force, making it ever more expensive. "Since September 2001," reported UPI Pentagon correspondent Pamela Hess, "the number of junior enlisted soldiers—the bulk of the Army, and on whose shoulders rest most of the fighting in Iraq and Afghanistan— has declined by nearly 20,000 total, according to Defense Department statistics. . . . There are now 4,000 more sergeants than recruits, privates and corporals put together. In 2001, there were 27,394 more junior enlisted troops than sergeants. . . . There were 97,119 sergeants in 2001. There are now 110,532."[19] Perhaps it's time to institute another index of military effectiveness, the ratio of generals to sergeants. Perhaps an Army can be "oversergeanted" as well as "ovengeneraled."

So there are good reasons why some people are staying: grade creep, wartime promotions, and bonuses, in addition to love of service and country. Fine by me. I wish all service people got paid a whole lot more. But these are unusual wartime promotions, accelerated not because people are getting killed and wounded so much as because people are getting out. Who can blame them, especially after they've done a tour or two? No one can be "good to go" all the time. People miss their families, want occasional normalcy, wear out. A 2005 RAND Corporation study confirmed the obvious. Exhaustion from too many deployments and worry over families, not avoidance of combat or arduous duty per se, drives people out.[20]

And now to the final problem. Neither the Army nor the other services determines how many people they can hire or keep. Congress does that by setting force levels and appropriating the necessary hundred billion plus a year, excluding veterans' benefits, which comes out of other accounts. But Congress does so within three sets of strictures. Short of major war, defense gets only so much of the federal budget, only so much of the gross domestic product. Over the past few decades, these have remained astonishingly stable: between 15 and 20 percent of the federal budget, between 3 and 4 percent of GDP.[21] Further, defense personnel costs generally don't rise above a certain percentage of the total budget, usually around 25 percent. Also, each service receives a roughly similar percentage of the total pot, about 30 percent each. As the most labor-intensive of the services, the Army traditionally spends the most of its allotment on people, often around 40 percent. But the service cannot meet its matériel replacement and modernization needs, let alone its "transformational" aspirations, while paying for people.

At least, it can't so long as the present allocations and percentages remain in effect.

So the Army, knowing full well the strain it will place on its present soldiery, has chosen to emphasize things over people. It has done so for a complex mix of reasons, some valid, some perilous. Yes, things take longer than people to develop and acquire. Yes, the American way of war rightly emphasizes high tech over bodies. Yes, the Army has recognized that, no matter how slick its advertising, it cannot garner enough quality recruits; it certainly can't offer enough to steal them from the other services. And yes, the Army, *rightly*, doesn't want to do any more Iraqs, and doesn't mind almost saying so, which it does by proclaiming its unwillingness to grow much beyond 500,000 souls.

And therein lies the peril. The Army's preferences, indeed the preference of the entire military establishment, may not accord with reality. The century-old Plans/Reality Mismatch is with us again. And this time, we may not be able to dodge it.

EVER SINCE AMERICA became a global power, people, or lack thereof, have been America's worst potential military shortfall. Few Americans know how lucky we got, again and again. Still, it matters to recall, if only to understand why, this time, we may not be so fortunate.

During World War I, American troopships and ships hauling supplies for the British and French went to Europe via different convoy routes. The Germans, disdainful of American fighting qualities and sensing correctly that American material support to the "Associated Powers," as Wilson insisted on calling them, would have more immediate impact than the doughboys, concentrated their submarines against the supply ships. Thus the entire American Expeditionary Force came ashore unmolested, and took only serious, European-style casualties for a few weeks in the spring and fall of 1918. What would have happened had the U-boat wolf packs struck the troopships and fifty thousand Americans died at sea? What would have happened had the German army chosen to fight on in November 1918, rather than going home to confront their domestic communists? At the very least, there would have been American horror at the carnage—and the discovery of how few men we really had.

During World War II, we raised only half the divisions originally deemed necessary—the Ninety Division Gamble. So by the summer of 1944, as the fighting intensified, we were effectively out of manpower. Had the atomic bomb not definitively gotten the Japanese government's attention, we would have invaded the home islands with troops who had already fought their way across Europe and the Pacific . . . while the Russians took on the main Japanese forces in China.

And manpower remained a problem throughout the Cold War. It was, simultaneously, a problem of too little and too much: too little in uniform to do what we said we would do, and far too many civilians to man the force we were willing to pay for. It was a problem redeemed only by nuclear weapons and bureaucratic fantasy.

While America poured its forces into Korea, including hundreds of thousands of recalled veterans, the 1951 NATO Lisbon Conference determined that there was no way the alliance could field an adequate conventional force against the Soviet Union. Nukes would have to substitute as deterrents or, deterrence failing, as "first use" firepower. Fortunately, deterrence worked. But from the 1950s on, the Pentagon engaged in a fantasy of such magnitude that, were an individual to run his life according to its dictates, he would likely find himself certifiable. Conventional force planning came down to justifying the maximum that Congress would allot while trying to squeeze out a bit more through a series of declaratory "strategies" as ludicrous as they were grandiose.

By the 1960s, Pentagon planning had settled on a two-and-a-half-war strategy—fighting simultaneous conventional wars against the Warsaw Pact and China, with a "half-war" somewhere else. The half-war that happened, Vietnam, effectively gutted the military for a decade. After Nixon opened China, planning shifted to a one-and-a-half-war strategy, a Warsaw Pact invasion of Europe plus a Korean fracas, with the additional post-1980 problem of a Soviet invasion of Iran.

Fantasy. Pure fantasy. The White House and Congress set the spending limits and that was what the military got, regardless of military plans or realities. The budget was the only reality that mattered. But the habit of fantasy segued into more insidious kinds of self-delusion. We never ever raised a fraction of the forces we needed. We never came close. I vividly remember one day in 1981, reporting to the Marine Forces command element headquarters of the old Rapid Deployment Joint Task Force at Camp Pendleton, for a reserve tour. I was handed a draft of RDJTF OPLAN 1001, which mapped out how the Army were to counter a Soviet invasion of Iran with maybe three American divisions. I was told to take it into the vault and read it. An hour later, I emerged and asked my colonel: "Sir, did they send you the joke issue by mistake?" The colonel, a tough old fighter pilot, only shrugged. The plan was so flawed that the Pentagon ultimately killed it. But it was not atypical. The Cold War's Ten/Ten Plan postulated four divisions stationed in Germany, with six more to fly over, draw their prestaged gear, and get into position within ten days of alert—to face fifty or more Warsaw Pact divisions, assuming the Soviets even let them land.

Jimmy Carter, inheritor of a thoroughly demoralized military that he did little to improve, played with a "swing" strategy, sometimes called Win-Hold-Win. American forces would win rapidly in one theater, wherever that might be, then "swing" to the other, where American forces were holding on gallantly, pending their arrival. Ronald Reagan had little use for such notions. He merely concentrated on building the force that would do Desert Storm, while leading the Soviet Union to a better understanding of the logic of their situation and the consequences of their ways.

As the Cold War faded the Bush Sr. administration engineered an orderly, across-the-board drawdown in active forces, while attempting to be able to expand, rapidly, should the need arise. Like Reagan, Bush the Elder had no time for nonsense. But nonsense could not be avoided forever, if only because the plan had each service take the same share of the cuts. This avoided the worst Pentagon civil war since the 1949 Revolt of the Admirals. But it also precluded serious decision making about how to handle the new world.

Throughout the Clinton years, the fantasy factory churned on, part the old games, part the unwillingness to start an interservice slugfest over roles, missions, and the budgets they generated. A series of official studies, now remembered mostly for their acronyms—BUR, CORM, QDR-1, NDP—maintained the fiction that American forces could fight two major regional conflicts (MRCs), in Korea and the Middle East, simultaneously. When this notion became too patently ridiculous even for the Pentagon, they responded by changing MRC to MTW, or major theater war, and dropped "simultaneous" for "overlapping time frames." Meanwhile, President Clinton took the 25 percent force reduction that the Bush Sr. administration had planned, turned it into a 40 percent cut, and essentially capped spending. He and his muscular humanitarians then used a shrunken, underfunded force more than any peacetime president before him: in Somalia, in Haiti, in Bosnia, in several dozen minor commitments, and in the skies over Iraq and Kosovo. People wore out and got out. The "recurring migration of funds" from procurement, maintenance, and R&D accounts to support current operations hollowed out the military.

During the 2000 presidential campaign, Bush Jr. and running mate Dick Cheney encapsulated their defense policy in one phrase: "Help is on the way." Donald Rumsfeld went to the Pentagon committed to a serious, rationally implemented "transformation"— military jargon for using high technology to create a twenty-first-century force invincible on any conventional battlefield, and capable of hitting most anything, anywhere, at will. He got off to a promising start, establishing a series of study groups, and refused to propose major budget increases until he knew what was needed.

The services, which had expected a Reagan-style "bow wave" of spending, were furious. Neocons even called for his resignation. Much depended on QDR-2, a congressionally mandated master blueprint, due out in the autumn of 2001. The services expected major changes, and were ready to rumble in defense of their budgets and missions.

Then came 9/11, Afghanistan, and Iraq. And those who wish to understand America's current declaratory strategy would do well to start by asking: What's the fantasy du jour?

WHEN PRESIDENT BUSH took office, total national security expenditures were around $400 billion, about $300 billion for the Defense Department, $100 billion for the rest: intelligence, nuclear weapons, border control, etc. Now they're pushing a trillion a year. In a January 2005 memo, Secretary Donald Rumsfeld urged the Pentagon's leadership to place defense spending in perspective, quoting the observation of the vice chairman of the Joint Chiefs of Staff, Admiral Edmund Giambastiani, that the United States spends the same share of its GDP on defense as Tanzania—that Tanzania's defense budget was \$20 million was also noted. Still, Secretary Rumsfeld called the GDP comparison an "instructive" alternative to merely counting the trillions.[22]

No matter. The big increases that might have gone to modernization and reform are gone. Transformation's a wreck, even though a lot of high-tech gadgetry has found its way to Iraq. Everybody's scrambling to save what they can. Meanwhile, the official strategy of the United States has raised the demands upon the military by orders of magnitude.

It is not that this new strategy is wrong, although in Iraq it has been wrongly implemented. It just cannot be executed with the forces available. And this time, there's no one to save us from our own unwillingness to pay for it, in treasure or in lives.

The Paperwork Reduction Act notwithstanding, the federal government loves paper. Indeed, there seems to be an iron rule at the Pentagon: The smaller the force, the greater the tonnage of documents about it. There are strategy white papers, annual reports, special reports, commission reports, studies, vision statements, road maps, posture statements, doctrines, endless others. Some actually matter.

After 9/11, it was generally assumed that the 2001 QDR would be a dead letter; some suggested that it be postponed indefinitely. QDR-2 came out on October 1, 2001. It did not fail to astonish. Or more precisely, it would have astonished . . . had America bothered to read it.

QDR-2 affirmed that homeland defense was now Job #1, and counterterrorism now a global endeavor. But it did not ditch the "two war" construct. In fact, it intensified it by suggesting that, henceforward, war would be prosecuted more aggressively. Prior to QDR-2, American strategy for conventional war had been to let the bad guys strike first, halt their advance, build up, then counterattack to restore an international border and negotiate a favorable peace. Now the goal was to "swiftly defeat aggression in overlapping major conflicts while preserving for the President the option to call for a decisive victory in one of these conflicts—including the possibility of regime change or occupation. . . ."[23]

Afghanistan got regime-changed. And in September 2002, the White House issued *The National Security Strategy of the United States of America*, setting forth President Bush's vision of the global future. The NSS is, in many ways, a moving and eloquent document. It correctly assesses the tenor of the twenty-first century, the fundamental quest for a greater fullness of humanity. "America," the NSS asserts, "must stand firmly for the nonnegotiable demands of human dignity: the rule of law; limits on the absolute power of the state; free speech; freedom of worship; equal justice; respect for women; religious and ethnic tolerance; and respect for private property." It notes correctly that "America is now threatened less by conquering states than we are by failing ones. We are menaced less by fleets and armies than by catastrophic technologies in the hands of the embittered few." And it pleads for a world where nobody has to live on two dollars a day.[24]

As for the military aspects of national security, QDR-2 affirmed that responses to aggression now went far beyond restoring borders. The NSS held that "We must adapt the concept of imminent threat to the capabilities and objectives of today's adversaries." Placing all the world's governments on notice that they would be held responsible for supporting terrorism, the NSS went on: "To forestall or prevent such hostile acts by our adversaries, the United States will, if necessary, act preemptively."[25]

Then came Iraq, and the slow discovery that while removing dictatorships was easy, replacing them with democracies could be hard. Along with that came the realization, as though it hadn't been known all along, that occupying countries, fighting insurgencies, and building nations were very people-intensive activities. High tech could take you only so far.

At issue here is not the decision to invade Iraq, which I opposed, or the right to take preemptive action, which I support as a general principle. Nor is the issue what may still be accomplished in Iraq, or whether it will prove worth the dollars and the lives. At issue here is the quantum expansion of the Plans/Reality Mismatch since 9/11— a mismatch that only grew in 2005. It's ironic that our greatest people shortfall in a hundred years comes not when facing the massed armies of totalitarianism, but against failed states and terrorist networks.

In the world of Pentagon paper, the White House NSS generates an amplifying document from the secretary of defense, *The National Defense Strategy of the United States of America*. The NDS in turn generates an amplifying document from the Joint Chiefs of Staff, *The National Military Strategy of the United States of America*, which helps the services run their own paper mills. The sequencing is rarely tidy. These papers, like babies, usually appear only when they're ready and sometimes it's unclear just what's begetting what. The March 2005 edition of the NDS codified America's post-9/11 military stance. In Pentagonese, it's known as "1421." First, as the NDS explains, it will "Defend the U.S. Homeland." Then it will "operate in and from four forward regions to assure allies and friends, dissuade competitors, and deter and counter aggression and coercion." Then it will "swiftly defeat adversaries in overlapping military campaigns while preserving for the President the option to call for a more decisive and enduring result in a single operation." Finally, it will "conduct a limited number of lesser contingencies."[26]

With what?

No matter that the document now speaks of "campaigns" instead of "wars" and of "adversaries" not "aggressors." No matter that the words "occupation" and "regime change" have been replaced by "a more enduring and decisive result." The question remains.

With what?

Still, we have learned one lesson from Iraq: Making the world safe for democracy requires the military to do more than break things and kill people. Eight months after bringing out the NDS, the Pentagon published "Department of Defense Directive 3000.05, Subject: Military Support for Stability, Security, Transition, and Reconstruction (SSTR) Operations." Henceforth, these activities, once known as "nation building" and eschewed by the military as a costly diversions from the task of fighting real—that is, conventional—wars, will be "a core U.S. military mission that the Department of Defense shall be prepared to conduct and support. They shall be given priority comparable to combat operations and be explicitly addressed and integrated across all DoD activities including doctrine, organizations, training, education, exercises, materiel, leadership, personnel, facilities, and planning."[27] And again:

With what?

There they went again.

The 2005 QDR, or QDR-3, came out on schedule in February 2006, thanks to an amendment to the 2003 National Defense Authorization Act, stating that the due date is "in the year following the year in which the review is conducted, but not later than the date on which the President submits the budget for the next fiscal year to Congress." The run-up to the publication proved a splendid exercise in deflating expectations. The Pentagon promised little; the analysts and the media expected even less. In January 2006, Deputy Defense Secretary Gordon England commissioned eight major "spin-off reviews," presumably to settle issues that the QDR left unaddressed or answered only partially. Included were subjects such as "Institutional Reform and Governance," "Irregular Warfare," and "Authorities." Thirty "lesser studies," originally intended to be complete by QDR time, would also continue.[28] Officials cautioned that this would not be a revolutionary, or even a transformational, document, but more of a midcourse correction. Perhaps Rebecca Christie of Dow Jones Newswires, or some anonymous editor, caught the gist of it in an article headlined, "Pentagon Study Dodges Questions, Gets Credit for Answers."[29]

As a road map for the future, QDR-3 wasn't wrong. It was merely delusional in its inability to relate strategy to resources, and plans to plausibility. It began by noting that the United States was now in the "fifth year of this global war" and throughout employed the phrase "long war," almost as a mantra. It then proceeded to a long list of "shift[s] of emphasis," including moves from "under-resourced standby forces (hollow units)—to fully equipped and fully manned forces (combat-ready units)." Included also, progress "from fragmented homeland assistance—to integrated homeland security," "from major conventional combat operations—to multiple irregular asymmetric operations," and "from forces that need to deconflict—to integrated, interdependent forces." (I add this last because, frankly, I have no idea what it means.)[30]

The rest of the document behaves, if that's the word, rather like a boasting barroom braggart whose assertions have been called into question. It alternates between increasingly ludicrous dominance posturing and occasional prudent, if subtle, back-stepping. The United States intends to remain "proactive" and help "shape the choices" of hostile and potentially hostile nations and groups. "In many cases," the QDR asserts, "actions must occur on many continents in countries with which the United States is not at war." To make the point again: "Long-duration, complex operations involving the U.S. military, other government agencies and international partners will be waged simultaneously in multiple countries around the world, relying on a combination of direct (visible) and indirect (clandestine) approaches."

Meanwhile, the Defense Department commits to doing whatever needs to be done by way of homeland security, which it defines as its absolute and unconditional first priority and urges Congress to eliminate caps on "pre-event spending," while also suggesting that it would like to minimize, over time, the resources committed.[31]

Having determined that the military would defend the homeland while pursuing terrorists anywhere and everywhere for the next few decades, the QDR then suggested that China seems to have embarked on a long-term military modernization, including "large investments in high-end, asymmetric military capabilities,

emphasizing electronic and cyber-warfare; counter-space operations; ballistic and cruise missiles; advanced integrated air defense
systems; next-generation torpedoes; advanced submarines; strategic nuclear strikes from modern sophisticated land- and sea-based
systems; and theater unmanned aerial vehicles for employment by
the Chinese military and for global export."[32]

Having defined the global war against terrorism and the emerging Chinese threat, the QDR distinguished between "steady-state"
and "surge" situations. Steady-state means the routine struggle.
The surge goal is to wage two nearly simultaneous conventional
campaigns (or one conventional campaign if already engaged in a
large-scale, long-duration irregular campaign), while selectively re-
inforcing deterrence against opportunistic acts of aggression. Be
prepared in one of the two campaigns to "remove a hostile regime,
destroy its military capacity, and set conditions for the transition
to, or for the restoration of, civil society." In order to do all this,
the document concludes that "the size of today's forces—both the
Active and Reserve Components across the Military Departments—
is appropriate to meet current and projected operational demands."[33]

Whence cometh this adequacy? The QDR posits three sources.
First, it redefines the "Total Force." This term, that once meant the
active/reserve uniformed mix, now includes "civilian and contractor
personnel."[34] Civilian employees, the vast majority nondeployable,
okay maybe. But "contractors"? The inclusion, which practically no
one noticed, suggests increased outsourcing of war to private military corporations, perhaps to foreign corporations and legions.
Many of these companies are staffed by former U.S. military personnel, maintain high ethical standards, and do good work, although some expanded too quickly for Iraq and took in too many
questionable characters, with predictable results. That they should
now be included as a significant part of America's "Total Force" indicates a disturbing trend that can be summarized by one distasteful
word: mercenary.

Beyond that, the QDR asserts that the United States is developing a new kind of soldier, superior to anyone ever fielded. The prose
is noteworthy.

"Future warriors will be as proficient in irregular operations, including counterinsurgency and stabilization operations, as they are
today in high-intensity combat. They will be modular in structure at
all levels, largely self-sustaining, and capable of operating both in
traditional formations as well as disaggregating into smaller, autonomous units. They will be able to sustain long-duration irregular
operations, while exploiting reach-back to non-deployed elements of
the force. They will understand foreign cultures and societies and
possess the ability to train, mentor, and advise foreign security forces
and conduct counterinsurgency campaigns. They will have increased
capabilities to conduct time-sensitive operations, by fusing intelligence and operations at the tactical level . . ."[35]

Noteworthy for its grandiose ludicrousness. The American soldier is not now, nor is he or she likely to become, either a multilin-
gual prodigy or a bionically engineered superwarrior. American
soldiers are among the world's best. They are not a new species.

Finally, the QDR recognizes that neither contractors nor Robo-
Cops will suffice to police, let alone dominate, the planet. Quality
matters, but quantity has a quality all its own. Therefore, the QDR
intends to increase, over the next several years, the Army's special
operations forces by a few thousand and add about 3,700 civil affairs
and psychological operations personnel . . . while *reducing* the
Army's active strength by about 15,000 soldiers (and cutting nearly
10,000 from the Marines).

QDR-3 lived down to its pre-publication expectations. Much of
the criticism centered on the disconnect between the document's aspirations and the defense budget Mr. Bush submitted a few days
later. Amazingly, only a few analysts mentioned, and then mostly *en
passant*, the people problem. Only Lawrence J. Korb, a former Reagan administration assistant secretary of defense and now a fellow
of the liberal Center for American Progress, issued an alternative

QDR, *Restoring American Military Power*. This progressive variant stated plainly: "The recruitment, training, development, and retention of quality military personnel must be the Pentagon's top priority." It recommended an active Army of at least 575,000, plus 500,000 in reserve.[36] He got it right.

A month after QDR-3 appeared, the White House issued its new *National Security Strategy*. The document, like its predecessor, was often moving. It said the right things about democracy, opportunity, dignity, and their enemies. It reaffirmed the American commitment to these values. Regarding military power, it noted only that the national security establishment was preparing to meet four kinds of challenges—traditional, irregular, catastrophic, and disruptive—and that "We fight our enemies abroad instead of waiting for them to arrive in our country."

Concluded President Bush: "Like the policies of Harry Truman and Ronald Reagan, our approach is idealistic about our national goals, and realistic about the means to achieve them."[37]

Mr. Bush not withstanding, the Plans/Reality Mismatch has never, *never* been greater. We expect to defend the homeland, defeat global terrorism, fight conventional wars, occupy and rebuild countries, improve the planet, win the Wars of the Ways or whatever they're calling it this week . . . with an imploding, overcommitted, and unaffordable military. Some would argue that it's time to bring our commitments into balance with our resources. But we cannot do that little. We dare not. The future of the planet may be at stake. The American future certainly is.

Meanwhile, we may take comfort in knowing that, as of this writing, the Defense Department plans on a basic budget of $2.3 trillion over the next five years. This will buy, as things stand now, fewer of everything, including people. The Army is thinking about cutting as many as 34,000 soldiers, mostly from the National Guard, while slowing its planned reorganization from divisions into brigade combat teams. They'll be lucky to stand up fifty, or to get their ultimate dream machine, the Future Combat System. Well over a decade into development, nobody's sure exactly what the FCS is, or will be. They hope to know by 2025.

Recruiting continues toward the goal of attracting about 160,000 new recruits—half for the active Army, half for the Guard and reserve—by October 2006. They're serious. According to Defense Secretary Donald Rumsfeld's 2005 *Annual Report to the President and the Congress:* "[T]he fiscal 2006 budget provides $1.6 billion for recruiting programs, which increases our recruiting force by over 3,000 recruiters (to 6,129 active, 1,774 Army Reserve, and 4,100 National Guard recruiters). The Army provides its recruiters the most up-to-date training to align them to their centers of influence and demographic trends in their areas. The Army has also increased College Fund grants to $70,000 for qualified active-component applicants and increased the maximum enlistment bonus from $8,000 to $10,000 for reserve-component, non-prior-service accessions."[38]

Not mentioned in the *Report*:

The Army wants to offer first-term enlistment bonuses as high as $40,000, and now pays reenlistment bonuses as high as $150,000, while the National Guard offers members a $2,000 "finder's fee" for each new member they help sign up. (They used to give out engraved Zippos.)

The Army has fired its old ad agency, Leo Burnett, and hired McCann-Erickson. Better ads are coming to attract young people and their "influencers."

Entry standards, from age to intelligence to high school diplomas to prior disciplinary problems are, in Pentagon parlance, "waiverable." The Army currently takes up to 4 percent "Cat IV's," the lowest acceptable mental category, made infamous by Robert McNamara's Vietnam-era Project Hundred Thousand experiment in giving such people uniforms and weapons, then hoping for the best. In October 2005, 12 percent of their active enlistments were Cat IV's; Army officials won't reveal how many they accepted in November. The service reports that Cat IV applications are now in "double digits."[39]

And there's a final reason why, since the beginning of fiscal 2006 last October, the Army has been meeting its quotas. In the manner of airlines maintaining their on-time percentages by lengthening the published duration of their flights, the Army has been lowering its quotas. When the *Christian Science Monitor* pointed out that the October and November 2005 quotas were smaller than a year before, Army Secretary Harvey sent off a letter, explaining that the numbers had not been lowered for the sake of cosmetic success. Rather:

"The Army modified its monthly goals . . . as a prudent measure to put our tracking system in line with the cyclic peaks and valleys of recruiting throughout the year. This practice is commonly done in industry: Monthly sales goals are established to reflect the cyclic nature of the specific market place."

He concluded: "Recruiting isn't just a challenge for the Army; it's a challenge to the nation."[40]

In that much, at least, he was right.

Coda

As of April 2006, the Army was meeting its quotas, and the National Guard exceeding theirs, through a set of interlocking manipulations. Standards continue to be lowered, in the sense of accepting more people who would have been turned down a few years ago. The most recent available statistics, for fiscal 2005, indicate that the Army granted 11,018 waivers of one kind or another, about 15 percent of total recruitment and up from fiscal 2004's 9,300 waivers, or 12 percent. Of these, 630 were for serious criminal misconduct, including "aggravated assault, robbery, vehicular manslaughter, receiving stolen property, and making terrorist threats," according to Douglas Smith, a spokesman for the Army Recruiting Command. There were 737 waivers for alcohol and illegal drugs and over 5,000 for medical conditions.[41]

The Army has also raised the maximum age to 40, liberalized its policy on tattoos, and eased up on boot camp. "The idea," says Col.

Edward Daly, commanding officer of a boot camp training brigade at Fort Leonard Wood, "is to get rid of the anxiety and worry."[42]

But if the quotas are being met . . . what of it? This year's, last year's, next year's—none have any real relevance to the need. A few thousand more or less, when the Army needs tens of thousands more. And that is the proof that the Army has given up on the American people. Not the statistics, not the waivers, not the bonuses, not the games, but the ongoing and willful refusal to admit, clearly and in public, that this Army is far too small for the tasks at hand. To put it into terms that most Americans can understand, the Army is living, people-wise, from paycheck to paycheck, and is only one lost paycheck away from disaster.

So why won't the Army admit it? Because to do so would mean invoking a word that, if taken seriously among other things, could wreck what's left of the Bush administration. That word is, "draft."

2

The Panic that Wasn't . . . or Was It?

THERE IS, in American public life, a process by which the unthinkable becomes the inevitable. An idea is floated. It is quickly derided, denigrated, dismissed, sneered off as impossible, impractical, absurd. Those with the power to enact or implement the idea deny that they have any intention of so doing, or ever will. The dismissals and denials keep coming.

But the idea does not go away. The media and the think tanks, the political spin machines and advocates, don't let it. Neither, in our enlightened era, do the bloggers and the Net. Strange alliances form, dissolve, then coalesce again, rather like companies that go bankrupt, only to start business anew under other names. In time, the idea enters the realm of the known, and therefore the potentially acceptable. This is how mass communication works. Gradually, the burden of proof shifts from those who would do something over to those who oppose it. The problem gets redefined as a crisis.

Sometimes it is. Then suddenly, or so it seems, the impossible becomes the new reality. We wonder how it came to pass. Then we wonder how the initial cost projections could have been so ludicrously low, and why the crisis doesn't go away, or why the solution to the crisis has generated other, maybe even worse dilemmas than those it was meant to alleviate.

This is how we got into Vietnam. This is how we got into Iraq. We may end up leaving the same way, as the idea of a quickie "declare honor and leave" exit takes hold and the burden of proof shifts to those who would have us stay. And this is how the Great Draft Panic of 2004 came and went . . . and remains. In truth, it wasn't much of a panic at all. Many have already consigned it to the status of an election-year urban legend, a product of political gamesmanship, misinterpreted documents, and far too many e-mails. Perhaps it was. But it was also a strange, taut exercise in national uneasiness, apprehension over who was fighting and dying in Iraq and who wasn't. Or perhaps it would be more accurate to call it a vague uneasiness over our national *lack* of uneasiness over who fights the wars we keep getting into.

True, a few columnists, such as the *New York Times*'s Bob Herbert (himself a former Army enlisted man) might run a minicampaign on the subject of "Sharing the Sacrifice, or Ending It."[1] Many would note, often with a certain gleeful contempt, that the children of the war's architects seemed to share their fathers' aversion to military service, and that President Bush's twin daughters would not be proceeding to the front any time soon. Some deconstructed their own conflicted emotions. Oren Rawls, a twenty-eight-year-old journalist identified as opinion editor of *The Forward*, a Jewish publication, considered himself "still young enough to whip myself into some kind of shape, if Uncle Sam so orders," and also declared his opposition to the war "a tad hollow—and will continue to do so as long as we're at war and I'm not serving." That he was the first male in three generations of family history "who has not had to strap on boots" left him carrying a significant load of "patriotic guilt" that, he admitted, he

had no intention of redeeming.[2] Meanwhile, Whitney Misch, a senior at Falls Church High School, a Virginia suburb of Washington,
D.C., asserted: "I don't want to die." The young man, described in a
Washington Post article as "clad all in black and with spiked, partially
dyed hair," warned America: "I don't know; I'd probably serve if I got
drafted, but it better not come to that. They better have some noncombat positions. . . . My future's too important to me."[3]

Well, yes. Not exactly a Light unto the Nations, but far from
hypocritical. Certainly not nearly as hypocritical as the young men
interviewed in Franklin Stevens's 1970 paean to draft evasion, *If
This Be Treason: Your Sons Tell Their Own Stories of Why They Won't
Fight for Their Country*. Certainly not as hypocritical as "Dick L.,"
who announced:

"My country presented me with a set of alternatives: to kill, to
go to jail, or to be dishonest. The fact that I chose dishonesty says as
much about my country as it does about me. Because, dammit, I
shouldn't have been presented with three almost equally unpalatable
alternatives.

"I feel it wasn't I who let my country down. My country let me
down."

The precise nature of this hypocrisy—and the larger question
of whether it was entirely hypocritical—will be considered later.
When Dick L. told his mother that his objection to Vietnam was
that "I *haven't been given a good enough reason* for fighting," he may
have been on to something quintessentially American and very contemporary. Whether another young man, who moaned that "It's a
terrible thing to bring a child into the world as a deferment," was
also on to something, we shall pass over in silence.[4]

Mr. Misch, who presumably has not enlisted, is safe now. The
draft hasn't happened. But the issue hasn't gone away. Perhaps it
should have, given President Bush's steadfast refusal to ask Americans for any kind of personal commitment to the war. Perhaps it
should, given the military and congressional refusal to create an adequate post-Iraq/post-Katrina military. But it won't go away. It

can't. It touches on too many profound political and moral issues. And in truth, the issue has been with us since conscription faded out, awaiting the moment when "problem" would be redefined as "crisis" and, in the manner of Washington, D.C., precipitous action taken, whether America likes it or needs it at all. Given current trends, it is not a possibility to be discounted or ignored.

To review the dilemma: Although this book opposes direct federal conscription, it also holds that the military should be much larger than it is. In technical terms, this is a matter of "force structure," of the art and science of creating armed forces. Force structure—and it's far more art than science—deals with everything from how many men are in an infantry squad to how many ships are in the fleet. It also involves endless trade-offs; there can never be enough money for everything. The United States must never lose its technological edge, especially against China and the weapons and defensive "asymmetrical systems" that QDR-3 noted the Chinese are developing and may well export. For example, the United States has long enjoyed aerospace supremacy. An enemy could deprive us of this by developing its own air force, or by concentrating on defensive measures such as electronic warfare and surface-to-air missiles. Some years ago, in a Navy war game, the Chinese took out the U.S. Seventh Fleet without ever putting a hull in the water; they did it with shore-based anti-ship missiles.

The high-tech edge must be maintained against future conventional contingencies. And high technology certainly has its place in the kinds of operations that the next few decades may routinely require. But much of the work, from domestic disaster relief to counterinsurgency and nation-building, requires people or, as the Army likes to say, "boots on the ground." Force structure involves trade-offs. But the things-versus-people trade-off has gone too far in the direction of things.

Fortunately, there is a way to correct this situation without a direct federal draft or massively increased expenditures—and without providing some future administration with the forces to do another

Iraq or two (something the Army justifiably fears). There is a force structure that is right for both the people and the military. Before discussing it, however, it's necessary to take a hard look at both the history of American conscription and the larger issue of the relationship of the people to the common defense.

WHEN THE DRAFT officially ended in 1973, conscription was generally regarded as part of America's "long national nightmare" (to borrow President Gerald Ford's apt phrasing from a couple of years later). It was an ugliness best forgotten, or at least left to molder away. It had been disposed of in typically Nixonian style. During the 1968 presidential campaign, Nixon promised to end the draft in much the same way as he promised to end the Vietnam war: vaguely. He then appointed a commission to study the problem. In Washington, D.C., commissions serve two purposes. If you don't want to do something, you appoint a commission. You then stack it with a toxic combination of insufferable status quo types and equally insufferable radicals, let them study the problem to death, thrash each other (makes it look like something's happening), thank them for their efforts, then forget all about it. However, if you want to do something, you name a commission that will tell you what you want to hear, then use the report to justify action.

The Gates Commission, officially the President's Commission on an All-Volunteer Force—the very name reveals the conclusion—reported out in February 1970, after Nixon and Ted Kennedy had already contrived to institute a draft lottery. After briefly addressing all the standard objections to a volunteer force, the Commission provided its fundamental reason to reject conscription. It was "a tax," an inequitable tax-in-kind levied on young males who were underpaid for their work. They thus accepted the reductionist view of economist and commission member Milton Friedman.[5] No need to argue anything else. Economics trumped everything.

(Ten years later, at a Hoover Institution conference on bringing back the draft, Friedman asked: "Are there any questions that are not at bottom economic?" A member of the audience, Richard Gabriel, a noted military writer, replied, "There had better be!")[6]

The new AVF, the All-Volunteer Force, America was assured, would be cheaper, better, and happier. And the youth of America, freed from the corrosive effects of coercion, would once again blossom with patriotic ardor and the spirit of service.

It didn't quite happen that way. As Vietnam and Watergate yielded to the Me Decade, pet rocks, Christopher Lasch's *Culture of Narcissism*, and President Jimmy Carter's homilies on "malaise," service did not become fashionable again. The AVF got off to a dismal start. Part of the problem was simple demographics. The baby-boom surplus was gradually yielding to the "baby bust" starting to come of military age in the late 1970s and 1980s. Another part of the problem was a significant decline in the quality of new recruits, as measured by the standard indices. In 1964, reported military sociologist Charles Moskos, the Army took in over 40,000 enlisted members with some college; in 1978, they accessed only 5,000. In 1964, 81 percent of draftees had high school diplomas, that key indicator of perseverance and discipline. By the late 1970s, only about 60 percent did, and many from the bottom half of their class in schools that specialized in adolescent warehousing, not education.

Another fact that makes you take Pentagon statistics with a certain tonnage of salt: In 1980, it was discovered that the ASVAB, the Armed Forces Vocational Aptitude Battery, had been "misnormed" at the lower end.

And that was how it was back then. All the services took such people as they could get, trained and disciplined them poorly, and kept many of them far too long. Everyone who served during those years has stories to tell, most often stories they rarely tell and would rather forget: tales of the confluence of Vietnam breakdown, ongoing racial tension, and institutional refusal to get serious about discipline and good order. I remember serving in a Marine Corps where every battalion had a de facto quota of special courts-martial, administrative discharges, and other disciplinary actions, all intended to keep the statistics presentable to Congress and the media. When General Louis Wilson, a World War II Medal of Honor winner, became commandant in 1977, one of his first priorities was to clean house. Disciplinary and discharge rates soared, which the media interpreted as the demise, not the resurrection, of, as one TV announcer put it, "the once proud Corps."

Political correctness didn't help. A fellow officer, serving as a battalion adjutant, told me of how a young Marine, on orders to Okinawa, walked into his office and explained that he belonged to a religious sect that forbade its members to go there. Something, apparently, of a negative pilgrimage. Processing the young man's objection took over a week. After personally seeing the lad onto the airplane, the lieutenant returned to the battalion headquarters, entered his colonel's office, and asked for the return of his application for augmentation from active reserve status into the regular forces. Said his commanding officer: "I don't blame you."

The Army fared worse, not least of all because, through years of ill-advised efforts to manage racial tensions by not confronting the radicals, they'd undercut the authority, credibility, and stature of a generation of African American noncommissioned officers. These men, who were damn good soldiers, either retired to the staff NCO clubs in disgust or got out entirely. Unable to attract enough good men, or keep enough good men to mentor them, the Army started bringing in more women (a subject to be considered in detail in Chapter Six). They also resorted, for the first time ever, to massive paid commercial advertising campaigns. No more cheapo "public service" ads. Madison Avenue found itself with a new set of megabucks accounts. Unfortunately, "Today's Army Wants to Join YOU!" didn't quite deliver. By 1979, results were so dismal that the General Accounting Office hired an outside marketing consultant to evaluate the effort. Their assessment: The problem isn't the promotion. The problem is the product. "If," the report concluded, "a similar situation were experienced in the private sector, it is quite possible advertising would be reduced until product improvements were made."[7] The Army's response was to launch the multi-megabucks "Be All You Can Be" campaign. By 1981, the situation had gotten so ludicrous that Bill Murray's hit movie *Stripes*, a kind of military *Animal House* about a misfit who squares away his basic training platoon while seducing female MPs in the general's house, could be viewed as sad military commentary as well as good-natured slapstick.

(The Marines, who also went to paid advertising, didn't make this mistake. One ad showed Gomer Pyle and his drill instructor, nose-to-nose above the caption "We Don't Promise You a Rose Garden.")

As the AVF got worse, it also got more expensive. Initial predictions of cost had foundered on three facts of AVF life. A volunteer, professional force had to be paid more, even if military pay failed dismally to keep up with 1970s inflation. A volunteer, professional force tended to be older and married-with-children, especially at the lower enlisted levels. This was new. The standard recruit was no longer the unattached young male who lived in the barracks (now known as the "bachelor enlisted quarters"), ate in the chow hall (now known as the "dining facility"), had no medical bills, and needed money only for leave, liberty, and vice. The emerging norm was the young family on food stamps.

Finally, there was the high cost of a "personnel turbulence," a bureaucratic euphemism for chaos. Washing out those new entrants who couldn't hack it (by some estimates, close to 100,000 per year), moving around the good people while dealing with the malingerers, misfits, and maniacs, ran up the tab. *Stripes* was one kind of commentary. By 1979, the prestigious *Atlantic Monthly* was running bring-back-the-draft articles by major writers such as the one by James Fallows entitled "Why the Country Needs It." Mr. Fallows, from whom we shall hear later, got right to the point. Quoting a

Washington Post letter to the editor that concluded: *"No. No. No. No. No. Never my child,"* he went on: "Nor my child, Mrs. Saylor. Nor either of my mother's sons when, ten years ago, both were classified I-A. But *whose*, then?"[8] So long as the military remained a peacetime "Armed Job Corps," the question need not arise. But everyone knew that the question would arise again. Especially if Ronald Reagan made it to the White House.

Ronald Reagan did make it to the White House. But except for a flurry of "AVF after Ten Years" analyses and a library shelf or two of books on the draft, the question did not arise.

President Reagan and his military leadership had three valid reasons for making sure it didn't. First, they weren't going to get a lot of good people, at least not immediately. Young men and women weren't waking up all over America, thinking, "Well, it's the Reagan years. Better go sign up." That took time.

Second, a new policy had completely changed the equation. The National Guard and service reserves, with some significant but small exceptions, had not been mobilized for Vietnam. The non-mobilization was part of LBJ's strategy for minimizing middle-class dissent by minimizing middle-class sacrifice, and had the effect of turning the Guard and reserves into middle-class havens from active duty. General Creighton Abrams, the Army's first post-Vietnam chief of staff, decided to restructure the service so that it could not engage in major or prolonged war without serious mobilization—that is, without the national commitment that made mobilization politically possible. This "Abrams Doctrine" had another benefit. Guard and reserve members cost only a fraction of full-time professionals. During the seventies and eighties, especially after the NPS (no prior service) draft-era guys got out, they also contained high percentages of Vietnam vets: men and women who kept up their military careers out of love. Further, the Guard and reserves contained many skills unaffordable to a peacetime army. Finally, reservists could quietly undertake missions that the regulars found either impossible or unpalatable, such as running refugee camps during the 1980 "Mariel Boatlift" out of Cuba. Those who entered the Guard and reserves during Vietnam may have been "weekend warriors." But many of those serving ten years later were not.

Under Reagan, the Abrams Doctrine was renamed the Total Force Policy and extended to all the services. Henceforward, the Guard and reserves would be deemed the full equivalent of the active forces. It worked well during Desert Storm. Perhaps too well. The notion that part-timers could accomplish so much did not appeal to the regulars. (Those old "Marine Corps Reserve: Your Job Is My Hobby" T-shirts that a few ill-advised Marine reservists wore to annoy the lifers may have had some truth to them. Politic, they were not.) The success of the Total Force Policy argued against a large post–Cold War Army, and the lifers were not averse to minimizing, one way or another, the accomplishments of the weekend warriors when it suited their purposes. Sadly, the Total Force Policy worked too well in another way. First under Clinton and then under Bush, it was expanded so far as to break the traditional covenant between the government and the citizen-soldiers. The implicit understanding was that they would be sent overseas only when clear national interests were in dire jeopardy, not for peace-keeping missions or wars of choice based upon flawed intelligence and a congressional Let's-give-him-the-power-and-then-get-out-of-town abdications.

The third and final reason why the Reagan administration was against raising force levels too much was that the RMA, or Revolution in Military Affairs, was getting under way. In essence, this was the confluence of all those new high-tech possibilities with some wondrous rethinking that had occurred during the seventies. The American way of war, according to historian Russell Weigley, had since the Civil War emphasized things over people. Throughout the 1970s, while the forces were languishing, a saving remnant of officers and civilians developed the enormous potential for a new way of conventional warfare, based upon precision-guided munitions, real-time intelligence, advanced communications, and a tactical/op-

erational doctrine known as "maneuver warfare." One happy consequence of the RMA was that, in future conventional wars at least,
fewer people need be hazarded to achieve spectacular results. The
money that became available in the early eighties could be spent on
things most justifiably. Another happy result was that the Soviet
Union, which had first understood the consequences of what they
called the MTR, or Military-Technological Revolution, was beginning to realize that it couldn't compete.[9]

Still, the issue of the draft did not entirely go away. Rather, it
got folded into the eternal quest, on the part of a few salivating liberals and some fewer disgruntled conservatives, for "national service
with military and nonmilitary options." The irrepressible Charlie
Moskos, who prefaced his 1988 book, *A Call to Civic Service*, with a
thank-you to his 1950s draft board for inducting him, and who is
still huckstering the concept today, kept it alive, along with a small
coterie of academics.[10] Not lost on them was the West German experience of using extremely liberal "alternative service" policies to
man their welfare state at minimal cost. National service, especially
the kind that would drive millions of young people into socially
"beneficial" activities, would be great social engineering. "The point
of all this," according to Moskos, "is simply that we the citizenry
and our political leadership must be attuned to thinking of how national needs might be met through youth serving their country and
community."[11] For-and-against anthologies, usually "for" but masquerading as fair, blossomed. They're still around. For example, two
students of the matter, Richard Danzig and Peter Szanton, presented their book as an exploration, neither for nor against. They
nonetheless decreed national service "an ideal" with many possible
variants. Others, especially communitarians and political scientists
concerned with loss of "community" (Amitai Etzioni and Robert
Putnam, to name two), have touted service as a wonder drug that
would accomplish everything from defending the country, changing
bedpans, and microfilming old library books to restoring patriotism,
citizenship, and America's essential cohesion.[12] Keeping in mind

Ayn Rand's dictum that whenever you hear anyone preaching sacrifice, there's usually someone else nearby collecting sacrificial offerings, all these plans and stratagems mostly reduce to:

1. A modest unconstitutional proposal for establishing a gargantuan teenager-herding bureaucracy to implement a form of age-based involuntary servitude that would disrupt lives
2. A requirement that young people perform such tasks as governmental social engineers decree
3. The accomplishment of little beyond the menial except for those in uniform
4. Engendering resentment
5. High cost, since administration is expensive, bureaucrats have to be paid, and since the youth so indentured would be paid twice—a modest or perhaps not-so-modest stipend while serving—then college benefits to keep America's preposterously overcostly higher education system at an even greater level of financial absurdity.

And there things stood for over thirty years, with conscription deader than week-old carrion, and about as aromatic. National service was only marginally less dead, taken seriously by a few specialized academics and a somewhat larger clique of advocates for doing on the cheap what the American welfare state had failed to do with untold trillions for over fifty years: provide all the services and other benefits they felt the American people deserved. And which they, or at least a few of them, hoped to help legislate and administer.

THE GREAT DRAFT Panic of 2004 had its origins in December 2002, when a liberal congressman introduced a bill he never intended to go anywhere. It ended in October 2004, when he voted against it. En passant, the panic, such as it was, provided a splendid opportunity to take a good look in the national mirror. America declined.

Representative Charles B. Rangel, a Manhattan Democrat who's been around for so long you almost believe "Congressman for Life" can be found in the Constitution, is a genuine hero of the Korean War. An African American, Rangel won the Bronze Star and Purple Heart at a time when black enlisted men could expect combat recognition to be rationed parsimoniously at best. In a December 31, 2002, *New York Times* op-ed, months before the Iraq war began, Congressman Rangel wrote: "I believe that if we are going to send our children to war, the governing principle must be that of shared sacrifice. . . . That's why I will ask Congress next week to consider and support legislation I will introduce to resume the military draft." After noting that only one member of Congress had, at that time, a child in the enlisted ranks, and that "Service in our nation's armed forces is no longer a common experience," he predicted: "There is no doubt that going to war against Iraq will severely strain military resources already burdened by a growing number of obligations. . . . We can expect the evolving global war on terrorism to drain our military resources even more, stretching them to the limit."[13]

Three days later, the *Times* quoted Rangel as hoping that the bill that he and Congressman John Conyers, another black Democrat, would soon introduce, "will help bring a greater appreciation of the consequences of decisions to go to war." "I think," predicted Rangel, "it's going to be a patriotic debate."[14]

HR 163, a bill requiring military or alternate civilian service of young men and women, was duly introduced, then referred to committee, where it was expected to remain forever. The Rangel proposal might as well have been stamped DOA. There was no significant debate, patriotic or otherwise. However, Caspar Weinberger, a former Reagan administration defense secretary and a decorated World War II veteran, did opine in the *Wall Street Journal* that the bill's House sponsors "have pushed some bad ideas before, but their proposal—to bring back the Vietnam era in the form of a military draft—is far and away the worst." Weinberger also accused them of "attempting to play both the race and class warfare cards" and of "utter and pernicious nonsense."[16] Weinberger did not mention that Senator Fritz Hollings of South Carolina, another decorated World War II veteran, was introducing identical legislation (S 89) in the Senate. Nor did Weinberger cast doubt on the motivations of Republican congressman Pete McCloskey, who won the Navy Cross as a Marine in Korea, for offering similar proposals in years past.[15] The issue at hand, according to Weinberger and many others, was less the draft than Rangel's opposition to the upcoming Iraq war. This was an adventure that, everyone understood, would be quick and cheap and easy. And who could possibly be against it on military grounds?

It was quick and easy and cheap—or so it seemed at first. There were, of course, a few indicators that all was not well, indicators apparent to anyone who cared to look. The Iraqi army, the Republican Guards, and the Special Republican Guard, had not been defeated. They had, except for a few encounters, merely disintegrated. A more determined resistance might well have prolonged the war for months, given emerging problems with the American logistical system. All that shock and awe notwithstanding, the Iraqi people had no sense that they'd been beaten so conclusively that their only choice was to submit to the Americans: liberators who were quickly turning into occupiers. Iraq 2003 was not France 1944. Few flowers, and far fewer female kisses, greeted the victors. And whatever happened to Saddam's arsenal? Not just the WMDs that never quite showed up, but the millions of small arms and munitions. Some that were indisputably real, the soldiers took home with them or sold. Others vanished from several dozen arms dumps. So serenely convinced were we of our invincibility and virtue in those first few months that neither the military nor the CPA, the Coalition Provisional Authority, considered them worth the trouble of guarding.

A year later, the original insurrectionaries, that motley crew of Ba'athist diehards, thugs, and crazies, had, by Pentagon estimates, already been killed several times over. But the insurgency and the potential for civil war kept growing, as did the Army's recruiting difficulties. And it began to dawn on the American people that there were bills already in Congress that could bring back the draft as soon as the spring of 2005.

The Rangel bill, and to a lesser extent the Hollings bill, provided a patina of credibility to growing suspicions that renewed conscription might be imminent. So did endless neocon demands for much larger forces, although those who wanted us to "cauldronize the Middle East" fastidiously avoided the dreaded D-word "draft." "We," insisted such no-prior-service stalwarts as Bill Kristol, Max Boot, and Frederick Kagan, could depend on "market mechanisms" to do it all, provided "we" had the "will." Their confidence was not universally shared. And when it got out that the Selective Service System was ramping up, or seemed to be, the balloon hit the fan for real.

According to *Time* magazine, the fun began in the spring of 2004 when a Pentagon Internet news service, defendamerica.mil, posted a routine notice from the Selective Service System that it was looking for unpaid civilian volunteers to staff up its 2,000 local draft boards. Normal attrition and all that. Even though the standard tour as an SSS local board member is twenty years, people do occasionally leave or die. SSS was and is in "deep standby," since the System's only ongoing function is to preside over draft registration. Still, bureaucracy must be served. Stories also circulated that Selective Service had been given an additional $28 million to prepare for a draft that could resume as early as spring 2005. In fact, no extra money had been appropriated. The total Selective Service budget for fiscal 2003 was $26 million; by their estimates, it would take at least $500 million to gear up. It would also take well over a year before any draftee could leave the United States, given the inevitable court challenges, the legal requirement that soldiers have at least three months of training before deployment. And the military reality is that at least six months are needed to produce a basic soldier.

Meanwhile, e-mails and reports circulated that the administration was indeed discussing resumption with SSS. These wandered and wended their ways through cyberspace, with predictable amplification.[16]

The White House, the Pentagon, and the Selective Service System all vehemently denied that there was any serious consideration of conscription under way. Yes, there had been meetings between the Pentagon and Selective Service to discuss the concept of a noncombat "skills draft"—computer people, Arabic linguists, truck drivers, that kind of thing. Documents had been generated. But nothing came of it, or was intended to. Just the usual contingency planning. Bureaucracy must be served.

No matter. The issue became a kind of inkblot test, wherein people saw what they were predisposed to see. Some Republican politicos and their surrogates considered the rumor just one more Democratic nasty trick. Congressman Curt Weldon, a Pennsylvania Republican, charged: "There is now a massive, politically based effort to scare our college students into thinking that somehow there is a secret plan by this administration to reinstate the draft."[17] Why Congressman Weldon limited the panic to college students is unclear, for America's high schoolers were getting just as freaked. Polls showed that a significant percentage of young people believed a draft was imminent. Web sites with names such as nodraftnoway.org and stopthedraftnow.com sprouted. Antiwar sites such as notinourname.net and moveon.org began devoting space and dudgeon to the issue. Pacifist sites such as the Quaker afsc.org, inisbco.org, and centeronconscience.org started offering guidance on how to "build your case" for conscientious objector status. Their universal advice: Start now, preferably after reading our handbook. A coalition of peace churches (Quaker, Mennonite, Brethren, etc.) announced that they would "coordinate their plans for 'alternative service' programs for conscientious objectors" in the event of a draft. As proof of possible resumption, they cited an unannounced visit by Cassandra Costley, SSS alternative service director, to the Brethren Service Center in Maryland. Selective Service said that Ms. Costley had dropped by simply because she was in the area and wanted to say hello.[18]

And Rangel's office, reported the *Wall Street Journal*, was besieged with complaints from people wanting to know "how he could get in bed with Bush" and do the administration's dirty work for them.[19]

As the 2004 campaign got under way, candidates of all persuasions hurried to distance themselves from the issue. Finally, in early October, the House of Representatives decided to take the kind of action that Congress takes when it wishes to settle something of no consequence with utter decisiveness. The Republican leadership suddenly called the bill out of committee and put it to a floor vote, for the purpose of defeating it. The final tally was 402 against the draft, two in favor. The two did not include Congressman Rangel, who in May 2005 reintroduced his legislation, to universal lack of notice and concern.

THERE IS, IN American public life, a condition that might best be described as peripherocentrism. You don't want to face the big issues, so you worry the little ones to death. It's a vital part of the process by which the unthinkable becomes the inevitable.

The Great Draft Panic of 2004 might have provided the opportunity to discuss a rather large issue: who goes to war, and who doesn't. America chose, instead, to elide and ignore and to fret the little stuff. Supporters of the Bush/neocon agenda contented themselves with demands for increases, without bothering to show where the money and the people might come from. Opponents of the war took on go-for-the-capillary issues such as banning recruiters from high school and college campuses or declaring their neighborhoods "recruiter-free zones." In 2005, San Francisco even passed a nonbinding and probably illegal proposition to that effect. But the fundamental issue—who serves and who doesn't—remains unaddressed.

In part, this is because it's a real-world nonissue. Those who do serve, all that blather about the "poverty draft" and "disproportionate casualties" notwithstanding, are indeed a cross section of America. It is not a strictly representative cross section. According to a September 2005 GAO report, the U.S. workforce is 71 percent white, while the military is 67 percent white. Blacks are overrepresented: 17 percent of the military but 11 percent of the civilian workforce. Hispanics are underrepresented, with 9 percent of the military and 11 percent of the civilian workforce. Are such small deviations from pure representativeness (whatever that is) significant? Not hardly. A bit more significant may be the fact that whites have accounted for 71 percent of the fatalities in Iraq and Afghanistan, with African Americans suffering 9 percent. Whatever else may be said of this force, it is not engaged in the wholesale wastage of minorities.[20]

Nor is it, as that old Civil War adage complained, a "rich man's war and a poor man's fight." Not exactly, anyway. The military does not collect detailed socioeconomic data on its entrants; that must be extrapolated in other ways. A standard technique is to take the zip codes of service members' "homes of record," where they officially report from, then match the zip codes with Census Bureau and other data on those areas. Here the picture is more complex and a great deal depends on how you define your parameters. For example, a Heritage Foundation study determined that 85 percent of recruits between 1999 and 2003 came from areas with household incomes between $30,000 and $200,000. Very impressive.[21] But another study by the National Priorities Project, using the same data, concluded that the large spread aggregates too many different classes and, as we all know, $200,000 buys a whole lot less in Manhattan, New York, than in Manhattan, Kansas. By a more detailed analysis, using counties as the relevant unit, the NPP study concluded that 64 percent of recruits came from areas with household incomes below the national median. But again, it all depends on what the money will buy you. Clearly, both studies work the data to suit their predilections.

Who's right? Both are. And neither. For the fundamental inability of this country even to face, let alone deal with, the matter of who serves and who doesn't is cultural, not statistical. It is a cultural problem impervious to statistics, to reason, even to an honest, open discussion. And it matters, in ways that far transcend the present dilemmas.

The American middle class, which once included everyone from unionized workers to professionals and executives, is fissuring. Part is rising. Part is falling. The reasons are many, from immigration and outsourcing to revivals of nepotism and the lunatic cost of higher education. This new class, not quite plutocratic but far wealthier and influential than the traditional middle order, has precious little contact with the military. Some disdain it. Many support it in the abstract, but as for sending their sons and daughters? Not Our Kind, dear. Probably the most affluent think about it as little as possible. If sufficiently pressed and persuaded to ignore the defensive PC mumble about "supporting the troops" (read here: don't disparage them too publicly), they would not respond with unmitigated enthusiasm. Yet these are the people who, for better or worse or until something major changes, determine much of this country's politics and culture. Books and articles about the military's alleged estrangement from civilian life and values have become common. Far less has appeared about the estrangement of this New Class, or whatever you care to call it, from the military and from service.

There is a reason for it: the legacy of Vietnam, now being passed down from the fathers and mothers to the sons and daughters. It's a complex legacy, in many ways bizarre. It's a mélange of omissions, distortions, and outright lies; a quest for unearned moral stature back then, a rigid refusal to judge that quest now. Vietnam is, in Freudian terms, "the return of the repressed." No matter how often we proclaim that the statute of limitations has expired, it hasn't. Nor will it, if the present generations of the Young Meritocracy continue to accept, often without knowing why, their parents' evasions and lies as some sort of superior morality.

Kathy Roth-Douquet and Frank Schaeffer understand this. In their book *AWOL: The Unexcused Absence of America's Upper Classes from Military Service—and How It Hurts Our Nation*, they return again and again to this theme.

"The Vietnam war," they write, "has become such a symbol of a deep divide in American political life that it will probably not be honestly or accurately assessed during the lifetimes of those Americans who were alive during both the war itself and the domestic battle in its aftermath. . . . in terms of how military service is perceived today by whole swaths of our population, Vietnam changed everything." They speak eloquently of an intellectual elite stuck in a legacy of mindless antimilitarism, and of protesters who will go to their graves unwilling or unable to reexamine their positions or their actions. And they yearn for a world where civic virtue and patriotism matter. "Our museums," they note, "are filled with portraits of the scions of leading families who led fateful charges," and "not so long ago, the sons and daughters of our political leaders served as a matter of course, as had their fathers before them."[23]

Indeed, they did. And *AWOL* bids, if not to get that world back, at least to reaffirm its value and get the upper orders' attention on the matter. The authors are speaking primarily to their peers, as much about their own conversion experiences as about the military.

Kathy Roth-Douquet started out as a nice Jewish girl. Shaker Heights, Ohio, daughter of a physician. Bryn Mawr, then graduate school at Princeton. Standard feminist shtick. She even got arrested once in a protest so scripted and so ludicrous that her mother asked to come along in the paddy wagon just for the experience. Liberal activism led to a job as a junior staffer in the Clinton White House.

Then she fell in love with a Marine. Ten years and two children later, her husband's a lieutenant colonel with two Iraq tours to his credit. She's changed her opinion on a lot of things.

So has her coauthor, whom she met at a book signing. Frank Schaeffer, a successful writer, never thought much about the military until his son enlisted in the Marines and went to Iraq. There followed three well-received books on the matter. *AWOL* provides a logical continuation of this fascination.

It's a book at once passionate and compassionate, personal and intimate without the usual cloying. It also provides an excellent primer on what the military does and an affirmation of service as an individual experience. It should be read and taken seriously.

But as I read it, and during my talks with Kathy, I kept sensing that something was missing. It is, of course, wrong to criticize authors for not doing what they never intended to do, and they made it clear that they had no intention of refighting Vietnam or its bizarre antiuniverse, the so-called Resistance. The effects of both are simply taken as given. And I kept sensing something else amiss: a glorification of the past at once too simple and too easy. It was as though they realized that going too deeply into the complexities would vitiate their message, which is to revalidate military service as an honorable and necessary calling. With that, I certainly have no quarrel.

But you can't get there from here. At least not without a clear understanding of just what the twentieth century, the century of the draft, meant to American concepts of military service and obligation, and how utterly different it turned out from what the Founders envisioned.

We start with two sets of rough statistics that, taken together, begin to unravel this tale. And I would emphasize that, when dealing with the draft, rough statistics are the best you're going to get.

According to President Ford's Clemency Commission, 26.8 million men turned draft age during the Vietnam era. Of these, 10.935 million wore a uniform in one capacity or another—about

41 percent. Only 3,250 went to prison for all draft-related offenses, including conscientious refusal to accept induction.

So, during the Vietnam era, *close to half of all eligible men served.* Serious, lay-it-on-the-line draft resistance was almost nonexistent.[24]

During World War II, according to Selective Service statistics, between November 1940 and September 1945, over 31.6 million men aged 18 to 44 registered for the draft. About 10.1 million were drafted. Nearly 4.9 million enlisted. Total: about 15 million, or close to 50 percent.[25] Not that much higher than the percentage of draft-age men who served during the Vietnam era, during the closest America has ever come to protracted total war. And even though there is one immediate, glaring difference between the Vietnam and World War II raw statistics—the Vietnam pool (ages 18–26) was one helluva lot younger and therefore smaller than the World War II pool (ages 18–45, with few over 40 drafted)—one similarity is equally glaring.

In each war, over half the service-eligible men did not serve. Whether we look at the Vietnam era, when there was an alleged surplus of Baby Boomer bodies available, or World War II, when the services were desperate for people, the percentage remains roughly the same. And, we shall find, for the same reasons.

I suggest here that the Vietnam experience with military service and evasion was not an aberration. Rather, it was the logical outcome of a conscription policy that has been remarkably consistent across the centuries. From the colonial period through the Civil War, and no matter how heroic and devoted the service of some, most Americans found ways to avoid it. Making it easy to avoid service has been government policy since the Civil War. The modern techniques were established during the First World War, codified during the Second, and carried over into Vietnam. There have been consistencies: corruption, bad faith, venality, incompetence, and failure. And until America understands these consistencies, and comes to terms once and for all with Vietnam's complex legacy, any talk about restoring military service to its rightful place in American life will be in vain.

And it matters to do so. In March 2005, six months after the House of Representatives had trashed the Rangel bill, the liberal *Washington Monthly* ran an article entitled "The Case for the Draft." The authors, an attorney/Army reserve officer/pundit named Phillip Carter and Paul Glastris, the magazine's editor in chief, stated their proposition clearly: "America has a choice. It can be the world's superpower, or it can maintain the current all-volunteer military, but it probably can't do both." They also stated their preferred guarantee that the American colossus will continue to bestride the globe: "the federal government would impose a requirement that no four-year college or university be allowed to accept a student, male or female, unless and until that student had completed a 12-month to two-year term of service." Options were civilian service, homeland security, or military as deployable noncombat specialists. Stipends and subsequent college benefits would be adjusted for length of service and degree of danger.[26]

My first reaction was: tenpins. Originally, bowling was done with nine pins, and called such. When the fathers of colonial New Amsterdam sought to improve the residents' virtue by banning ninepin as a waste of time, the pastime's devotees added a tenth pin and made it clear that they could add (or subtract) pins faster than the government could pass laws.

Four-year colleges and universities? How about five? Or seven? Or ten?

But more to the point: Sometimes freedom begins when you say *No!* to those who presume to tell you what your choices are. As for retaining superpower status, perhaps it should be said that what we do with it now might be more important than whether or not we keep it forever. Which we won't.

3

Conscription Corrupts

"LIES, DAMNED LIES, and statistics" was Winston Churchill's knowing quip concerning three of humanity's favorite techniques for ordering its behaviors, beliefs, and affairs. When dealing with statistics on military service and conscription, things can get damnable indeed, and not just because it's always easier to determine how many served than how many didn't, or why. There are, in essence, four major problems to address before proceeding.

The first is, of course, time. Records from the seventeenth through nineteenth centuries are sketchy at best, with the probable exception of the Union's Civil War records. An additional problem is the decentralized nature of twentieth-century conscription. The military gave help-wanted numbers to the Selective Service System, who translated these into geographical quotas, based upon available bodies and other considerations, sometimes political, sometimes administrative. Local record-keeping and reporting could vary tremendously in accuracy. Also, after any war, there's a normal human tendency to let the bookkeeping slide, and to engage in mass destruction of records, authorized or not.

When dealing with national draft statistics, that old computer maxim, GIGO—garbage in, garbage out—pertains.

Computers might have solved part of this problem, but as a matter of policy, they didn't. General Lewis B. Hershey, the director of Selective Service from World War II until Nixon fired him in February 1970, just didn't believe in them. Right up to the end, he resisted any equipment more complex than an adding machine. As he explained during one congressional hearing:

"I have had about four or five surveys made, and it is very plain, they say to me, 'If you want to run a decentralized system we can't do much for you with the computer. If you let us have a centralized system we will let the computers make the mistakes rather than the human beings.' I personally am sticking with people." When asked if he wanted any "data gadgets," he replied: "Well, I believe that we ought to use everything we can, but when we get into the sort of machinery that starts using us and that we begin to restrict what we can do because it won't go into the machine . . ."[1]

One suspects that this was more than mere geriatric Luddism on General Hershey's part. He very likely didn't want too much information available—to the Congress or the media.

The third dilemma in using statistics to get an accurate picture is that Selective Service regulations and procedures were constantly changing and guidance to local boards was often vague and contradictory. What might get you a deferment or an exemption in 1942 or 1965, wouldn't work in 1944 or 1969. Also, young men moved many times from category to category; by most estimates, three quarters of Selective Service's work involved making administrative changes in registrants' status—by hand. Lack of adequate full-time staff at the local-board level meant major sloppiness.

And finally, there was everything that, for one reason or another, never got written down, or was lost or destroyed. The more you look at this system, the more convinced you become that so many of the inequities and abuses can never be documented because they never were documented to begin with.

What the statistics, however rough they might be, actually reveal is that close to the same percentage of men of draft age served in Vietnam as in World War II—*less than half*. The percentage holds even when matters such as changes in the number of years a man was liable are factored in. This indicates a major continuity across the decades and the generations, regardless of anything else.

At first glance, the fact that less than half of all military-age males served during World War II, or any other war, might merit all the regard of a Pentagon press release on how well Army recruiting has been going of late. Three reasons to discount come to mind immediately, applicable to World War II (and World War I) and Vietnam.

Certainly a percentage will always be physically disqualified. But how are those standards set? As a rule, peacetime standards are much higher than in wartime, when troops are always in short supply. But the United States has always assumed that if a man is medically unfit for combat, he should be exempted from all service. This lets a lot of people off. Naturally, there were a lot of changes within this blanket policy. For example, during World War II, certain medical standards, notably vision and dental, were progressively relaxed. And during two brief periods, men were taken for "limited duty." Still, the fundamental principle remained. Such medical standards offered those desirous of avoiding service certain, shall we say, opportunities to do so. It was a way of defusing, of buying off, potential opposition under the guise of military requirements.

As for letting people off for mental reasons, we'll discuss in a bit the strange confluence of forces that made mental screening such an easy way to play the evasion game, from the First World War through Vietnam.

And what were the consequences of another kind of moral

judgment, that husbands and fathers should not be drafted? These were on-again/off-again deferments, depending on need and politics. But there were other dodges a man could use, such as claiming family hardship or finding war-related civilian employment.

If setting extremely high physical and mental standards constituted one standing invitation to play the game, and if deferring husbands and fathers offered another, industry and technology provided a third. War in the twentieth century was a time of mass economic as well as military mobilization. Millions of men and women were required for the fields and factories, the labs and railroads, and other vital functions. But how is it determined what's essential, and by whom, and who gets to fill those jobs? How many military-age men would the economic war effort require when older men were available and women by the millions were entering the workforce?

Contrary to popular belief, neither Congress nor Selective Service ever automatically exempted entire classes of workers. It was always up to the individual to apply, and in marginal cases to convince the local board that he was engaged in vital war-related work. Again, this vagueness offered major opportunities to play the system. And again, these opportunities served to defuse political opposition.

There were also numerous special categories, numerically small but politically significant. Exemptions for clergy and divinity students, or at least for those of conventional faiths, offered yet another exit. Among the reasons for the Catholic Church's current shortage of priests is the number of guys who went in to dodge the draft only to discover, sometimes in midlife, that this was not the way they wished to spend their earthly span of years.

More politically volatile and numerically significant was racism. The military was segregated until 1947, and a strange situation pertained. As a rule, it was much harder for poor African Americans to obtain deferments and exemptions. While physical and mental disqualifications could be had, hardship exemptions were extremely difficult to come by. After all, many African Americans would be making more in the service than at home. Deferments for vital war-related civilian work were scarce, even for block farmers. Most important, local boards back then were almost entirely white, and nobody was looking too closely at what they did.

But if blacks were often drafted in situations where whites might not be, the Army didn't really want them. In both wars, the Army set quotas for colored troops, to be used for noncombat duty only, and those quotas were not high. Arguments against the military's full acceptance of African Americans ranged from putative inferior intelligence and educational levels to lack of acceptance by whites. Then there was my personal favorite dodge: Blacks were by nature both too docile and too violent, too compliant and too rebellious to serve, let alone fight.[2] This policy more or less continued throughout the war, even as America's military manpower ran out in 1944. By 1945, black troops finally began to prove their worth in combat, in segregated units and alongside whites whenever field commanders became sufficiently desperate. General George Marshall, the Army chief of staff, knew segregation was wrong, but decided that justice would have to wait until after the war. It waited for a long time after that, but today it is fair to say that the military is the most successfully integrated profession, and society, in America.

Homosexuals were another special category. World War II was the first war in which homosexuality was treated as cause for exclusion, although anecdotal evidence indicates that far more gays lied about it to get in than told the truth to stay out. The reason for the exclusion: a bargain between the Pentagon and a coterie of psychiatrists, led by Harry Stack Sullivan, himself a closet gay. When the war started, the last thing military planners wanted to deal with was a large prison population. But homosexual acts were crimes under the Articles of War and the Navy regs, the old "Rocks and Shoals," precursors of the present Uniform Code of Military Justice, and the planners knew there would inevitably be a number of homosexuals serving. There would also be millions of scared young men, deprived of female companionship and vulnerable to temptations that they might not ever succumb to in civilian life. Dr. Sullivan, for his part, wanted homosexuality decriminalized and reclassified as a psychiatric disorder. So they struck a deal. Homosexuality would be made grounds for rejection, while first-time offenders in uniform would be treated as medical, not criminal, problems.[3]

Screening was duly instituted, and the screeners quickly learned not to ask "Do you like girls?" Even the most ardent homosexual could answer honestly that he did indeed "like" them. Other questions fared scarcely better, as in:

"Do you go out with girls?"

"No, sir."

"Why not?"

"My wife won't let me."

Such games notwithstanding, the homosexual exclusion policy remains in effect today under the formula that Charles Moskos provided the military. "Don't Ask. Don't Tell." And it will remain in effect until enough people ask whether it's the American way to exclude entire groups on the basis of what some might do, or on the basis of whether others disapprove of or dislike them.[4]

If it is indeed true that less than half of the eligible men served in World War II and Vietnam, they were able to evade service because of a system that made it incredibly easy to do so. Naturally, the fact that less than half served says nothing about the unique quality of America's World War II experience, or the Greatest Generation's accomplishments. And it was a unique experience. All told, over 16 million wore a uniform during those years. About 15 million were draft-age men. Over 400,000 were women, while the rest were presumably men past draft age: the senior officers and noncoms, the old professionals. The U.S. population back then numbered about 120 million. Virtually everyone had someone special in uniform. People cared.

And there was unity. Save for a few individual miscreants and absolute conscientious objectors, and members of absolute-refusal sects such as the Jehovah's Witnesses, everyone wanted to contribute something. Convicts did war work and even volunteered for medical experiments. Thousands of men with religious objections to war served in noncombatant roles, such as medics. One, Desmond Doss, won the Congressional Medal of Honor. Over 12,000 conscientious objectors not in uniform did significant work through the CPS, the Civilian Public Service program, unpaid and supported by various church and peace organizations. Some conscientious objectors took on hazardous tasks, such as "smoke jumping"—parachuting into forests to fight fires. Others, legitimately exempt, made their own separate peace with their conditions. Lee Iacocca, the legendary president of Ford and subsequent savior of Chrysler, was medically exempt due to a near-fatal bout of childhood rheumatic fever. A working-class young man, nearly all his male friends from high school were overseas. He went to college to study engineering and he was, as he recounts, "in no mood to goof off."[5]

Nam, this was not.

But the issue here is not military service. The issue is federal conscription, as it was practiced from 1917 to 1970. It was not universal, although that word sometimes appeared in authorizing legislation and in mendacious PR. Nor was it random, in the sense of "The lottery assigns your number and when it comes up, you go." The closest America ever came to this system was the final years of Vietnam, when draft calls were dropping precipitously—162,746 in 1970, 646 in 1973—and many boards were engaged in settling scores with prior troublemakers and evaders, and also playing their usual games, before dipping into that year's pool.

Rather, twentieth-century conscription was "Selective Service," which meant that somebody was establishing the categories of selectivity and somebody else was doing the selecting, based upon their own interpretations of what those regulations and guidelines meant. Militarily, the purpose of the system was to provide men. Politically and culturally, the purpose of the system was, in equal measure, to maintain civilian social stability, to practice social engineering, and to defuse tensions and resentment and opposition by making sure one helluva lotta guys *stayed out*.

Again, the issue here is not military service, or the accomplishments and sacrifices of the tens of millions who have served. Those matters are transcendent. The question under consideration is corruption by design, and the price we're still paying for it today.

And it's worth mentioning that there was one other fundamental difference between World War II and Vietnam that we're still paying for. If you had dodged the draft during World War II, when it was over, you shut up about it. If you dodged the draft during Vietnam, you're still talking about it, perhaps even bragging. That, too, has skewed the American understanding of conscription, and of America itself.

THERE IS AN interpretation of federal conscription that sees nothing either unusual or un-American about the draft. By this reckoning, conscription was (and is) just one more way to reify a millennia-old concept of citizen military obligation. From the Greeks and Romans through the Anglo-Saxon *fyrd*, the feudal proto-militia; from the colonists and Minutemen and Yanks and Rebs to the doughboys and GIs and grunts: a straight line. Sometimes you need it. Sometimes you don't. But it's all fundamentally the same thing. One way or another, when duty calls, you go. By this reckoning, America's military history is largely the counterpoint of two approaches. There were times when we had the draft, and times when we only talked about it.

We talked about it a great deal. The wartime correspondence of His Excellency, G. Washington is filled with demands and pleas and the direst of warnings to the Continental Congress that unless they provided a large permanent force, or adequate state militia contingents, or *something*, disaster would ensue. Only direct federal conscription, he finally concluded, would avail. There would never be enough money to hire a serious army. Volunteers came. Volunteers, save for a couple thousand (maybe less) "for the duration" types, went. The states rarely delivered the quotas Washington requested and the Congress only recommended; it had no power to compel. Sometimes the states preferred to keep their militias at home. Sometimes the militias did, too, and declined the opportunity to serve with the national army. The situation was desperate. The situation was usually desperate.

Washington's correspondence illustrated this wartime progression of despair. In a letter to Congress dated September 24, 1776, while his army was getting whupped in New York on a regular basis, he wrote:

"The Jealousies of a standing Army, and the Evils to be apprehended from one, are remote; and in my judgment, situated and circumstanced as we are, not at all to be dreaded; but the consequence of wanting one . . . is certain and inevitable Ruin. . . ." His plea for 50,000 or 100,000 "men in constant pay" (he had at the time maybe 20,000, and that was shrinking rapidly) was, of necessity, ignored. Only Europeans had money for armies like that.[6]

Two years later, having despaired of getting anything resembling a professional force, and of improving such troops as came his way, he wrote Congress. "If experience has demonstrated that little more can be done by voluntary inlistments, some other mode must be concerted, and no other presents itself, than that of filling the regiments by drafts from the Militia." He was willing to compromise. "As drafting for the war, or for a term of years, would probably be disgusting and dangerous, perhaps impracticable, I would propose an annual draft of men. . . ."[7]

Even as late as 1780, he would complain to Patrick Henry: "What remains for us to do? Nothing less than furnishing our full quota of Continental Troops by any means, that will ensure success."[8]

Most historians attribute this consistent congressional refusal and/or inability to a combination of poverty (the Congress couldn't tax the people directly), provincial self-concern, and fear of creating a "standing army" that might usurp power. Whatever the mix of reasons, America never fielded a genuinely adequate army. And it may have as much to do with Washington's character as with money, provincial fretting, or philosophical quibbles with standing armies.

George Washington was the Revolution's indispensable man. Everyone knew it, including George Washington. And everyone, including George Washington, knew that he was also a lousy field commander. This was a problem, inasmuch as he took the British rather personally. As a young man on duty during the French and Indian Wars, he'd coveted a regular commission in the British army. This they declined to provide. Colonials didn't rate it, so Washington had to content himself with a colonelcy in the Virginia militia. He never forgot the perceived insult and lusted to go against the redcoats for real in an eighteenth-century-style climactic engagement. Congress knew (as did Washington in his calmer moments) that the proper strategy was not to try to best them in a single, grand, and vindicating battle or campaign. It was to keep the army in existence, winning small victories while avoiding disastrous defeats, until the French bestirred themselves and the British wearied. Congress never gave Washington sufficient forces to attempt the showdown that he himself knew should not happen until the end, preferably with the French making up for Continental deficiencies. This happened. Nine decades later, Robert E. Lee would not be as lucky.

After the constitutional settlement, discussed in more detail later, the next time conscription got considered was during the War of 1812.[9] Nothing came of it, save for providing Daniel Webster, then a congressmen, yet one more chance for the kind of stentorian oratory that compels a new appreciation of sound bites. On December 9, 1812, Webster took to the House floor to oppose a proposal by Secretary of War James Monroe that urged conscripting individuals, for the first time, directly into the federal forces. As citizens of the United States, the reasoning ran, they should be as liable to federal as to compulsory state militia service.

"I have risen on this occasion, with anxious and painful emotions," Webster assured his listeners and, as always, posterity, "to add my admonition to what has been said by others. Admonition and remonstrance, I am aware, are not acceptable strains. They are duties of unpleasant performance. But they are, in my judgment, the duties which the condition of a falling state imposes. They are duties which sink deep in his conscience, who believes it probable that they may be the last services which he may be able to render to the Government of his Country. On the issue of this discussion, I believe the fate of this Government may rest. . . . A crisis has at last arrived, to which the course of things has long tended, and which may be decisive upon the happiness of present and future generations. . . . I am anxious, above all things, to stand acquitted before God, and my own conscience, and in the public judgments, of all participations in the Counsels, which have brought us to the present condition, and which now threaten the dissolution of the Government."

Having made it clear that the War of 1812 was about far more than getting Andy Jackson's picture on the twenty-dollar bill or even smiting the Brits, Congressman Webster got down to the matter at hand. The Monroe proposal was:

"[A]n attempt to exercise the power of forcing the free men of this country into the ranks of an army, for the general purpose of war, under color of military service. . . . Persons thus taken by force, and put into an army, may be compelled to serve there, during the war, or for life. They may be put on any service, at home or abroad, for defense or for invasion, according to the will and pleasure of Government. This power does not grow out of any invasion of the country, or even out of a state of war. It belongs to Government at all times. . . . Is this, Sir, consistent with the character of a free Government? Is this civil liberty? Is this the real character of our Constitution? No, Sir, indeed it is not. The Constitution is libelled, foully libelled. . . . Where is it written in the Constitution, in what article or section is it contained, that you may take children from their parents, and compel them to fight the battles of any war, in which the folly or the wickedness of Government may engage it?"[10]

The matter at hand was the invasion of Canada. The administration had tried to conquer the place, or at least get a chunk of it and maybe a favorable regime change. It wasn't working. Money was running out. The people weren't signing on. Congressman Webster concluded that if the citizens of the United States, simply by virtue of their citizenship, could be drafted to go redeem Canada, they could be drafted for any reason. Nothing in American history, custom, or law mandated such a notion. But something in the French experience did.

On August 23, 1793, the revolutionary French government decreed a *levée en masse* to defend the country against the invading armies of monarchical Europe. Its words, perhaps more than any other military pronouncement of the eighteenth century, foretold the future: total war.

"Henceforth, until the enemies have been driven from the territory of the Republic, the French people [*tous les Français*] are in permanent requisition for army service. The young men shall go to battle; the married men shall forge arms and transport provisions; the women shall make tents and clothes, and shall serve in the hospitals; the children shall turn old linen into lint; the old men shall repair to the public places, to stimulate the courage of the warriors and preach the unity of the Republic and the hatred of kings."[11]

This was new. For the first time in European history, submission to conscription became, in historian Daniel Moran's words, "a form of personal virtue." That which had once been odious and tyrannical, now became a high expression of democratic citizenship and patriotic ardor. Simultaneously, the old-fashioned voluntarism and service arrangements that had once been a "social process" were now assumed by the state, as a matter of fiat.[12]

After some initial and astonishing successes, the *levée en masse* demonstrated once again that even the most idealistic hordes need serious leadership. Napoleon provided it. In his hands the mass army became both the liberator of Europe and its oppressor. However disappointing the Corsican impresario turned out to be to American well-wishers and advanced thinkers, he certainly demonstrated what a nation-state could accomplish when it could draw without limit upon its people for whatever reasons it chose. The lesson was not lost upon the young United States, or upon members of its military establishment, even though the nation had at that time no need for mass armies.

History is a retrodictive affair. Looking back, it proclaims, "Yes, that's how it had to be." By most American reckonings, the War of 1812 was an afterthought of two eras, the revolutionary and the Napoleonic. It was a military escapade of little long-term significance, except that we finally stopped fighting the Brits and would not again consider conquering Canada until the late twentieth century, when films such as *South Park* and *Wag the Dog* had their seasons.

But in the end, maybe ole Dan Webster got it right. For the first time, America considered conscripting its citizens for whatever purposes the government desired. For the first time, America tasted that kind of temptation. Webster didn't go along. Neither did those states that withheld their militias, or who established their own state armies, or who considered withholding taxes from the federal government.[13] But America would succumb to that temptation a half century later, when its survival did indeed depend on how many millions it could throw into the field, how many scores of thousands it could waste.

Civil War conscription would prove a military and political mess. Mass armies would not. They were the future. And a few years after Appomattox, America watched with unabashed delight as Prussia's conscript army, having bested the Danes and the Austrians, smashed the French and unified Germany. Mass armies worked. And when they were used as the "school of the nation," acculturating its members to disciplined patriotism . . . that, too, could have American uses.[14]

. . .

IN 1866, AS in 1946, if you had contrived to avoid wartime service, you kept quiet about it. But certain veterans of the Civil War had something else to not talk about. Few draftees cared to admit that they'd been drafted. If it didn't carry a total stigma, it did indicate, or seem to indicate, that there was something lacking in your patriotism and probably something amiss in your skull. How could you let yourself get *drafted*?

Few did, at least in the North. Between July 1863 and April 1865, the federal government held four national drafts, calling up a total of 776,829 men. Of these, only 46,347 actually served, or about 5 percent.[15] The Union draft proved such a screw-up, and such an irritant, in so many ways that when the Wilson administration and the War Department began gearing up for 1917 conscription, they consciously used the Civil War experience as a model of how not to do it.

When the war began in 1861, both sides were flooded with volunteers, hoping for a quick and elegant victory. By the end of the year, it was clear that this was going to be a long, ugly slugfest. It was also clear that the vast majority of those who were going to volunteer had already done so. As for the young men coming up behind them, it was obvious—it's always obvious—that the longer the casualty lists, the less the ardor to hasten the process of adding one's name to them.

The Confederacy drafted first. That a government so dedicated to states' rights and the freedom of individual (white) citizens should resort to national conscription bespeaks a certain sense of realism: the realism of those who find themselves in impossible situations. The Confederacy had started the war without a national army, although it had no lack of qualified officers who'd left the federal forces. The Confederate Congress called out the state militias for six months while accepting national volunteers for one-year enlistments. These were not enough to fight against a resource-superior North that would ultimately adopt a strategy of "annihilation"—of defeating the rebellion so soundly that they dare never try it again.

The Conscription Act of April 1862 declared every able-bodied white male between eighteen and thirty-five subject to military service. The immediate and intended impact was to hold the 1861 volunteers, whose terms were expiring, in service for two more years. In 1864, as their three-year terms were expiring, the Confederate Congress passed a new law, keeping them on for the duration.

For those who had not yet answered the call, and didn't care to, substitutions were allowed. As Albert Moore, a southern historian writing more than eighty years ago, describes the process:

"The person employing the substitute accompanied him to the camp of instruction where he was enrolled, if found to be lawfully exempt [an inductee couldn't hire potential inductee to take his place] from military duty and pronounced by the surgeon to be in all respects fit for service. Then the former, the 'principal' so-called, was given a certificate of discharge by the commandant of the camp." The 1862 market price of a substitute quickly reached $3,000 Confederate; by 1863, $10,000 or several hundred dollars in gold. Some unenthusiastic potential soldiers started throwing in land as well.[16] Some substitutes became good soldiers. Other found the experience so profitable that they deserted and tried their luck again elsewhere. The substitution system became so corrupt and inefficient that, after several attempts at reform, the Confederacy finally abolished it. Then in 1864, the Confederacy decreed all white men seventeen to fifty available. By 1865, they were offering emancipation to slaves who fought. Yet until relatively late in the war, the South also exempted, by legislation and by policy, dozens of categories of men, from large slaveholders to mail contractors. The stay-at-home gentry proved especially galling to lower-class Confederate volunteers, most of whom were fighting, as one rebel prisoner told a Union officer, "Because you're down here."

It is impossible to state how many men were actually drafted, or how many of those served. Disintegrating governments generally aren't too particular about their record-keeping. A couple hundred thousand might be a reasonable guesstimate.[17]

The North got into the game with the Enrollment Act of 1863. As John Whiteclay Chambers points out, the law avoided all mention of the state militia system and provided for "enrolling and calling out 'the national forces.' This was an entirely new term and concept."[18] Daniel Webster's great fear was now law. Draft liability was decreed for all able-bodied male citizens and declarant immigrants (those who'd announced their intention to become citizens) between the ages of twenty and forty-five. Unlike the South, there were few statutory exemptions. There were, however, ample provisions for substitution. There was also commutation: buying your way out with a $300 fee that might then be used to pay enlistment and reenlistment bonuses to volunteers, at least until the practice was abolished in 1864. Also, notes Chambers:

"[T]he law created a powerful conscription agency. . . . In a land where the only federal presence had been an occasional postman or customs clerk, the act authorized the army to assign provost marshals to be in charge of the draft in every congressional district. These officers (who as military police were also charged with apprehending deserters and arresting suspected Confederate informants and spies) were authorized to conduct door-to-door registration, hold lotteries to select potential draftees, and induct eligible conscripts. Claims for exemption would be decided by an 'enrollment board,' composed of a provost marshal, a physician, and a third person, appointed by the president. Contrary to the traditions of American jurisprudence, the decisions of these boards were considered to be final; they could not be appealed."[19]

Writes historian James Geary: "In its final form, the Enrollment Act reflected Congress's desire to make the federal draft as acceptable as possible to Northern citizens while instituting the principle of universal liability to military service."[20] It's hard to tell whether Geary is being ironic or that Congress was being, even by congressional standards, exceptionally obtuse. The combination of easy evasion (for those who could raise the money) and heavy-handed administration could not have been better designed to antagonize people. In the summer of 1863, draft riots, the worst in American history, hit New York and other cities. True, issues beyond conscription were involved; rather often in riot situations, immediate grievances serve more as an excuse than a cause. Still, the distinction may have been lost on those six regiments marching back from the Battle of Gettysburg who found themselves on riot duty in Manhattan.

How effective was the draft at meeting national manpower needs? Directly, a total mess. Geary's statistics, drawn from the postwar *Final Report to the Secretary of War by the Provost Marshal General*, tell the sorry tale.

As already noted, over 776,000 men were called. Over 161,000 failed to report. Of those who did, nearly 207,000 were examined and held to service. Of those held to service, nearly 87,000 paid their commutation and over 73,000 furnished a substitute. The law made no explicit provision for conscientious objection. An unknown number were imprisoned, until the provost marshal general, apparently not wishing to add to the prison population, paroled them "until called for." This was, in essence, a de facto exemption. Others were forcibly taken to the field, where they joined the statistical category of "draftee."

So, of the 776,829 men ordered to report for examination, 46,347 were actually conscripted into the Army. By Geary's estimate, direct conscripts comprised all of 3.7 percent of all federal troops.[21]

The Supreme Court never ruled on the constitutionality of conscription, although Chief Justice Roger B. Taney wrote a private manuscript that deemed it illegal, mostly as a matter of states' rights.[22] But the principle that men may be conscripted directly by the federal government into federal service had been established—and just as quickly forgotten.

The veterans, as they would after World War II, quickly moved into positions of power and prominence in the nation's politics, business, and saloons. If you had contrived to evade service, you kept quiet about it. In one way, that was too bad. I would love to know what happened to the gent in Ohio who, when summoned for induction, gave his occupation as "bird fancier." Records indicate that he was exempted from service. Was bird fancying essential to the preservation of the Union?[23] And what of the other hundreds of thousands of stories of draft evaders and their families, now lost forever?

THE NATION SOON reverted to its "traditional" defenses: a small standing army, adequate to conduct wars of expansion/genocide on the western frontier while manning the arsenals and garrisons; special volunteers when needed; and a state militia system. This last, increasingly known as the National Guard, would gain formal recognition as the nation's militia by the Dick Act of 1903, and given enhanced federal status by the National Defense Acts of 1916 and 1920. However, many units spent the post–Civil War decades evolving into something less imposing: a congeries of middle-class social clubs, veterans' hangouts, and strike-busters. Such activities notwithstanding, the Spanish-American War seemingly vindicated the notion of the citizen-soldier. Militia units and special volunteers such as Teddy Roosevelt's Rough Riders performed well, or at least flamboyantly, while the regular Army revealed a combination of lethargy and incompetence that occasioned some serious attempts at postwar reform. But while the system was getting patched, the confluence of two other factors began to reconfigure conscription's future possibilities. When the United States entered World War I, conscription would not be sprung upon a people unaware or unprepared for it.

The French levée en masse of 1793, plus subsequent Napoleonic conscriptions and some German popular uprisings toward the end of that era, had shown very clearly the latent powers of the nation-state. When Prussian general and military strategist Carl von Clausewitz described modern war-making as a "remarkable trinity" of the army, the state, and the people, he had reason. The Prussian army, which had studied the American Civil War thoroughly, showed what was possible when mass armies were armed with mass-produced Industrial Age weapons, moved about on railroads, and were employed with competence and daring. By the early twentieth century, the major powers of Europe had adopted what became known, variously, as the expandable, expansible, or cadre-conscript model. Mass armies were essential, but large standing armies cost. The solution was to run conscripts through one to three years of active service, then assign them to local reserve units for the next decade or two or three, available for mobilization as needed. An additional benefit for newly unified nations such as Germany and Italy, and polyglots such as Austria-Hungary: Military service would serve as schools of patriotism, overcoming provincial loyalties. And discipline—read here: the creation of properly docile, non-Marxist worker and peasant classes—would carry over into civilian life back home.

The cadre-conscript model held great appeal to a certain class of American officers, especially those not overenamored of the militia and its loosey-goosey ways. Unfortunately for these "Uptonians" (named after Emory Upton, an intellectual guru of the movement), America had no military use for a large army. Still, to at least a few influential officers and civilians, it did have other uses.

The "preparedness movement" of 1915–1916 is often viewed as part activist statement, part joke: middle- and upper-class young (and sometimes not so young) men attending military summer camps at their own expense, drilling under Army supervision of varying degrees of rigor. A twenty-first-century American might view the whole "Plattsburg" phenomenon (name of one of the major training sites) as little more than fantasy camps. But in truth, the movement had started decades before, and had a certain Progressive era earnestness about it.

Good Progressives, at least some good Progressives, always (or at least sometimes) tried to meld the best of three worlds:

twentieth-century efficiency and power, the regulatory and amelio-
rating enthusiasms of government, and nineteenth-century values,
especially those of individual autonomy and character. To many, especially Teddy Roosevelt and his old Rough Rider comrade,
Leonard Wood, a Harvard-trained physician who ended up as Army
chief of staff, war provided a special blend. But wars were hard to
come by for the average American in the early twentieth century,
unless you wanted to suppress Filipino guerrillas, smite Chinese
rebels, or straighten out a Latino nation or two. Not everyone did.
However, brief Universal Military Training (UMT), six months or
so, could be salvific. At least, General Wood believed so. UMT, he
held, would both provide a large semitrained reserve manpower
pool and make the army "a greater mill through which the population is passed." Mill, melting pot, same principle. All those immigrants, so many of whom had come to the United States to avoid
military service, would be rendered patriotic and disciplined, and
trained to accept the orders of their natural superiors, the young
WASP officers from places like Harvard and Yale. The military goal
was the creation of a modern army, American-style, not exactly a
European arrangement, but close enough. However, few regular officers shared his enthusiasm. As they saw it, soldiering was best left
to long-term professionals. The last thing they wanted was a semitrained semirabble, consuming scarce resources or even worse—a
citizen-soldiery fully capable of learning in a few months what took
the regulars years. But General Wood's agenda was as much social as
military, and in his social agenda he found some ardent and well-
placed civilian allies.

The social and cultural goals were, as military and cultural historian Michael Pearlman put it, "To make democracy safe for America."[24] Perhaps it would not be amiss to suggest that the draft was
drafted into this cause, and provided the vocabulary, if not the reality, by which future demands for conscription would be justified. It
was a complex affair, with four discernible aspects.

The first, and probably least important, was the eugenics craze:

an enthusiasm not unknown to even the most benevolent Progressives. This opined that universal service would, in time of war, prevent the deterioration of the national gene pool. As Munroe Smith, professor of comparative jurisprudence at Columbia University, explained: "If modern war makes in any case for the survival of the physically unfit, modern war waged by volunteer armies makes for the survival of the socially unfit."[25] The marginal and the mediocre would be given opportunities to serve the country by fighting and, hopefully, by dying.

Second, the quest for universal military training received support from medical men, albeit in a rather convoluted way. Medicine was struggling to establish itself as a scientific endeavor, and would play an ever-increasing role in the nation's military life, starting in 1917. But before the war, it viewed universal military training as a badly needed dose of old-time religion. Scientific medicine had adopted the "germ theory" of disease, the notion that sickness is caused by microscopic organisms. But Leonard Wood, a nonpracticing physician of the old school, along with many others clung to "Christian pathology," the belief that sickness was divine punishment for sin or, as we might put it today, bad choices and an unhealthy lifestyle. Historically, no one had ever claimed that military life—the life of disease-infested camps and trenches and brothels—was healthy, let alone salvific. Now medical men did, often portraying military training as the Boy Scouts writ large, or at least a logical extension thereof. It was physically healthy for young urban males especially, getting them out of the slums, at least for a while.

But it was also seen as a way of building character. Opined Dr. Charles W. Burr, Professor of Mental Diseases at the University of Pennsylvania:

"Unless the American boy is taught obedience, unless he learns to submit to authority, unless he learns that the highest ideal of manhood is to obey, unless he learns that work is a blessing, this country is doomed. . . . Universal military training will do much to stiffen up, to make firm-fibered and manly the boys of America."[26]

George Creel, a friend of Wilson's and director of the wartime Committee on Pubic Information, which made advertising the *leitmotif* of the cultural war effort (his postwar memoir was entitled *How We Advertised America*), agreed. "Universal training will jumble the boys of America all together, shoulder to shoulder, smashing all [*sic*] class distinctions that now divide and promoting a real brand of democracy!" He even suggested that conscription would regenerate "the heart, liver, and kidneys of America," which he felt were in "sad need of overhauling."[27]

The clear subtext here was, training was good for the poor, especially the immigrant poor. And thus the third allure: social stability. But the burden of stability did not fall entirely on the new arrivals. Indeed, the fourth aspect of the pre–World War I push for universal military training was that the elites were losing it and, without their regeneration, little else mattered.

The quest for the physical and moral toughening of the upper orders began as something of a fad. An enterprising gent named William Muldoon ran a spartan, military-style health camp for the rich and well-connected. He may not have coined the terms "military therapeutics" and "martial medicine," but he was certainly an apostle of "No pain no gain." So deeply did he and his customers believe in the value of painful exercise that one of his most popular rituals involved men throwing a very large, very heavy sphere, that he called a "medicine ball," at one another. But it took General Wood to get the army involved. It began in 1913, when the army sponsored a summer camp for men who paid their own way . . . and who performed surprisingly well under the benign tutelage of some of the service's more ardent drill masters. Concluded Pearlman: The Plattsburg Movement (named after the first camp in New York) gave its recruits the chance to get whipped into physical and moral shape while "aton[ing] for the riches they kept." It was all part of the great Progressive dream of "solv[ing] America's social problems without redistributing its wealth and power."[28]

Prior to 1914, the UMT movement had both its benign and its

ludicrous aspects; it was essentially harmless. But as World War I sunk into the trenches, the old American question, "Preparedness for what?" now seemed to have found its answer. Wood had finished his term as chief of staff and now served as commanding general of the Army's Eastern Department, which conveniently included the centers of American urban power, New York and Boston, especially. Wood and his old friend, Teddy Roosevelt, began pushing preparedness in earnest. But the vital impetus came from Grenville Clark, then a young and well-connected New York lawyer and fellow Harvard alum, a WASP poster boy if ever there was one. In November 1914, Clark had written Roosevelt about a "little scheme" he had to "get organized a small military reserve corps composed of young businessmen, lawyers, etc., who would go through a very light sort of training to fit themselves to be of some use in case of any real emergency."[29] The Military Training Camps Association formed and by 1916, both college students and, as Clark liked to put it, "tired businessmen," were going through the camps by the thousands. What had begun as personal therapy would soon be dreadfully real.

By 1917, the pieces were in place. The Civil War had established the principle of direct federal conscription. The Progressive Era added the notion that compulsory military service is physically and morally good for the individual, especially the urban individual, and a fine piece of social engineering. It remained for Woodrow Wilson to provide the war.

When war erupted in August 1914, the United States had no good reason to intervene, and no power to do so. America also had plenty of reasons to stay out. The violation of Belgium notwithstanding, this was just one more depraved old-world squabble. Over one third of the nation were either immigrants or the children of immigrants; even in those families of more lengthy residence, old loyalties and animosities still brewed. If few German Americans wanted to fight Germany, probably even fewer Irish wanted to fight for England. Escapees from eastern and southern Europe showed scant desire to fight for, or against, Italy or Austria or Russia. Better just to trade and preach. Indeed, two years into the war, after repeated violations and outrages by the Germans, and lesser but still real British depredations against American shipping, Wilson could still win reelection on the slogan "He kept us out of war." And among the top ten hits of that year, at least when measured by sheet music sales, was a number entitled "I Didn't Raise My Boy to Be a Soldier."

Preparedness advocates might put forth as gospel the notion that army life was good for you. But Mother wasn't buying it.

At what point Wilson decided that he couldn't keep us out of war is unknown. It's possible that by 1917 his decision-making was already affected by the forces that would lead to his stroke in 1919. A personal sense tells me something else. By 1917, the war had become a catastrophe looking for redemptive reasons. The European belligerents, especially France and Germany, kept escalating their war aims, promising their exhausted peoples anything to keep them going. Wilson was also looking for reasons that would justify exposing America to the carnage. Ultimately, he decided that the only justification would be a complete reversal and renewal of human history, via American arms. He would make this the War to End War, with himself as presiding savior. He meant it.

But how to sell it? I've often suspected—where are the opinion polls when you really need them?—that American support for the war was 3,000 miles wide and 6 inches deep. Pundits then and historians since speak of "war hysteria," as though a declaration by Congress tripped some sort of switch in the national psyche and America ran amok until the switch got flipped back in 1919. True, journalists and historians can study only that which is visible to them, and you never hear about the lynchings and riots and lunacies that don't happen. Nor is it widely acknowledged how often this war, like the Civil War draft and the Pearl Harbor attack, provided racists and other lowlifes with the occasion to act upon preexisting animosities. But so much of what is visible was the product of Wilson's decision to privatize coercion while selling the war as the domain of a great people and a righteous government.

The key word is "selling." And the draft was so marketed, not as coercion but as exemplar of all that was right with America. It was to be a new kind of draft, democratic yet efficient. It also ensured that the American people would find plenty of ways to dodge service.

A declaration of war, it should be noted, does not actually oblige a nation to do anything. It merely proclaims that certain legal and political conditions now exist. And if it is true that you fight in war the way you trained in peace, it is also true that people do not abandon their deep-set habits, or their decencies, just because there's a war an ocean away. The problem is, how to get them to act as though they have? A good commercial does not rationally persuade. It simply asks the consumer to suspend rationality, at least long enough to buy the product. And as every CEO knows, the better your advertising and PR, the less you ought to believe it.

By 1917, it was clear that Woodrow Wilson had bought his own advertising. It was the end of a long process of self-persuasion. In the summer of 1916, Wilson was already thinking about raising an army.[30] Viscerally, he favored voluntarism. Viscerally, he also hated it. His archnemesis, former president Teddy Roosevelt, was hyperactive in the preparedness campaign. TR was also publicly saying things about Wilson's character that, were the roles and their lines reversed, would have caused Teddy to provoke the first duel (or at least middle-aged brawl) between a sitting and a former president. Intellectually, Wilson favored selective service as the modern, Progressive way to rationally allocate manpower while disrupting the civilian economy and society as little as possible. Still, he was torn. As war approached, he swung once toward the old way of raising an army of "U.S. Volunteers," but probably dropped it because TR was talking about raising a division under his personal command.

(As the tale goes, after the war started, Roosevelt finally visited

Wilson, asking for permission to raise his own division. Wilson politely but firmly declined. On his way out afterward, Roosevelt ex-
claimed tearfully to Wilson aide Colonel Edward House, "Doesn't
he know I'm just asking for permission to die?" House allegedly responded on the order of, "Are you sure you made that clear?")

In any event, planning for conscription proceeded during the
early months of 1917 with no public fanfare, and the bill was not
presented to Congress until after the declaration of war. As another
tale goes, Major Palmer Pierce, an aide to Secretary of War Newton Baker, was testifying before the Senate Finance Committee
shortly after the declaration, when he mentioned that "we may have
to have an army in France."

Astonished committee chairman Thomas S. Martin interjected,
"Good Lord! You're not going to send soldiers over there, are
you?"[31]

Popular historian Mark Sullivan captured the national mood after the declaration a bit better. "Vaguely," he wrote, "but only
vaguely as yet, America realized that war on Germany involved
something more grim than the thrill of hearing the declaration.
Somebody must fight the war."[32]

Neither Wilson nor Congress waited until the enthusiasm of
the first volunteers subsided. The bill was passed a few days after the
declaration of war and the Selective Service System went into operation in May 1917.

In several ways, it was profoundly different from its Civil War
predecessor. While the War Department maintained overall control,
the work would be done by local civilian boards that would be given
general guidance and quotas, but not much more. This was classic
Progressive gamesmanship: presenting exercises in federal power as
affirmations of local autonomy, democracy, and values. (The American Medical Association had sold medicine to America the same way,
keying on the small, independent practitioner who just happened to
enjoy a state-sanctioned professional monopoly.) However, the
downside of this reliance on "little groups of neighbors," a system

that would last until 1973, was obvious. Everything depended on the character and honesty of the board members. Opportunities for favoritism and venality, corruption and the settling of old scores, and about as many other agendas as the mind can conceive, were ubiquitous. Board decisions were not final; there was an appeals entry into a far from sympathetic judicial system. But who knows how many millions upon millions of acts of preference or bigotry or vengeance were committed; how many files got lost or found; how many lives and relationships were ruined.

Still, localism was a convenient safety valve to limit animus against the war or the federal government. If there was injustice, blame it on the board.

Commutation and substitution were abolished. The actual legislation mandated very few exemptions, mostly for government officials, clergy, and divinity students. But the law authorized the executive branch great leeway in creating its own deferment and exemption categories, especially regarding essential war work. This they did, although usually without specific guidance to local boards. At first, marriage and fatherhood were grounds for excusal. And for decades thereafter, journalists and historians took great delight in noting how many people discovered true love before each draft call, and how many babies resulted from these unions.

In addition to marriage and dependency deferments, students found that they could avoid service overseas by signing on. The Student Army Training Corps (SATC) permitted about 145,000 young men to serve in uniform as college students: the ancestor of several World War II college-in-uniform programs that had to be shut down in 1944 when manpower ran out.

One final, magnificent dodge was made available to the young men of America, although not quite intentionally. As noted already, the prewar UMT movement relied heavily on medical endorsements. As Pearlman put it, "When Wood sought to mobilize a constituency for universal military training after 1912, he received support from numerous doctors who apparently possessed more faith in the therapeutic efficacy of army service than most professionals ever had. In 1916, for example, seventy-nine presidents of state medical associations, nineteen presidents of national medical societies, ten chairmen of American Medical Association divisions, and representatives of ninety-five medical schools went on record for universal military training."[33] Not surprisingly, when war came in April 1917, several thousand physicians, usually too old for military service, volunteered to do local draft-board medical screening. The Army would set the standards and there would be a second medical exam after inductees reported for service. But in a pattern that would prevail until 1973, the judgment of a local physician that a man was medically unfit for service was rarely questioned, save by those eager to serve. If the examining physician was also a man of stature in his community, his word was even more likely to be final.

Obviously, this raises the possibility of favoritism and abetting potential draft dodgers in individual cases. But physicians as a profession had another reason for rejecting large numbers of young men.

Medicine was not quite yet respectable, its claims to scientific stature still not accepted. As a profession, it had a vested interest in demonstrating to America just how sick it really was, that is, how greatly in need of their ministrations. This dovetailed nicely with the Army's desire to minimize active-duty health problems, and the government's inclination to keep postwar veterans' expenses to a minimum. So the doctors found, not surprisingly, that America was far less healthy than anyone knew. Tens of thousands of young men were turned away for ailments they'd never heard of, or that had never hindered them in civilian life. One wonders how many later sought out the examining physician for treatment.

The contribution of the nation's psychologists and psychiatrists, two groups also determined to prove that America needed their ministrations far more than America knew, were even more energetic. What happened here is far from common knowledge, since research and popular concern have centered on psychology and psychiatry's ministrations to people in uniform, not the pre-entry screening process. Still, what these two groups did to the war effort is fascinating.

Among the psychologists, Robert M. Yerkes took the lead. An early behaviorist, he held that science should concern itself only with those aspects of human mental function that can be scientifically observed and measured, i.e., behavior. This school also claimed for itself a scientific ability to manipulate behavior. Indeed behaviorism's American godfather, John B. Watson, made a fine career for himself on Madison Avenue, after getting fired from Johns Hopkins University over an affair with a teaching assistant. Yerkes was imbued with Watson's insights. He was also a recognized expert on primates. When American entered the war, he was president of the American Psychological Association, and in a good position to offer his profession's services to the war effort. The gift he bore: intelligence testing. He pushed the idea with such gusto that detractors and even neutral observers came to wonder if, as one historian puts it, "he was more concerned with performing a vast intelligence testing experiment than with aiding the war effort."[34] Yerkes and his colleagues quickly devised two short intelligence tests, one for those who could read, one for illiterates. Ultimately, the Army consented to test everybody, soldiers as well as potential inductees. The tests showed conclusively that whites were smarter than blacks, and western and northern Europeans had better brains than those from southern and eastern Europe. And tens of thousands of young American men were exempted from military service because they'd been classified as morons.

The Army approved, more or less. Prior to the war, it had given little institutional thought to the intelligence levels of prospective soldiers, preferring to emphasize "character," meaning mostly an acceptable level of vice. It found in the psychologists a convenient way of minimizing its own personnel hardships, even if it had scant use for the psychologists' professional claims. At any rate, testing for intelligence was a far less volatile issue than weeding out those who might be susceptible to what had become known as "shell shock." And that involved not the psychologists, but the psychiatrists.

If medicine got scant respect before the twentieth century, psychiatry got even less. Psychiatrists mostly ministered to the unfortunate, usually impoverished residents of state mental hospitals, or to middle-class crazy aunts and ladies with the vapors. Sigmund Freud's scandalous obsession with *"la chose sexuelle"* didn't help. And although early twentieth-century medicine could point to some wondrous accomplishments, psychiatry had little to show.

From the psychiatric point of view, World War I provided one gigantic laboratory of madness. And military psychiatry was born, in large measure, to struggle with the debilitating effects of combat and hardship on the human psyche. Not surprisingly, the army wanted to minimize its problems in this area by pre-induction screening. Perhaps one American psychiatrist, Dr. John T. MacCurdy, expressed the desired result best when he wrote in 1918 that:

"In conclusion it may be well to speak briefly of means that may be taken to prevent in future such terrible strains being made on the efficiency of fighting forces as the neuroses have produced in all the armies at present at war. The first method which naturally comes to mind is the removal at the time of enlistment of all men who are not adapted to fighting . . . the ideal soldier must be more or less of a natural butcher, a man who can easily submit to the domination of intellectual inferiors. . . . No one of course who is ill-adapted to civilian life at the time of enlistment should be considered."[35]

So much for the therapeutic effects of service.

How many young men actually got out of service on such grounds? Impossible to say. But it's safe to conclude that, as the war ran on and more and more thousands of American soldiers succumbed mentally to the horrors of war, both the opportunities and the reasons to avail oneself of the opportunities increased.

Thus the system. But there remained the matter of getting potential draftees to present themselves in the first place. During the Civil War, army officers had gone door to door, seeking eligible men. Now it was decided that the young men of America should register for service voluntarily, and that Registration Day should be touted as a patriotic carnival, not a grim and somber act that could lead to death, physical disability, or insanity for hundreds of thousands. "'I am exceedingly anxious,' [secretary of war] Newton D. Baker wrote the President, 'to have the registration and selection by draft conducted under such circumstances as to create a strong patriotic feeling and relieve as far as possible the prejudice which remains to some extent in the popular mind against the draft by reason of Civil War memories. With this end in view, I am using a vast number of agencies throughout the country to make the day of registration a festival and patriotic occasion.' "[36] George Creel, ever anxious to oblige, turned his "Four-Minute Men" (volunteers who gave standardized short speeches to boost morale) to the task of hyping "Universal Service by Selective Draft." (Lest anyone consider this a minor effort, Creel reported after the war that his 75,000 Four-Minute Men had delivered a total of 7,555,190 speeches to over 300 million people.)[37]

Stanford University historian Paul Kennedy sums it up best when he writes that, "the purposefully dramatic cultivation of intense emotion became nevertheless a cardinal method in the operation of the military draft, as did official encouragement of vigilante activity aimed at non-registrants and 'slackers.'" This for a draft whose ostensible purpose "was to serve primarily as a way to keep the right men in the right jobs at home," an intense campaign of official PR and privatized coercion so that the government could, as Wilson put it, simply make a selection from a people who had already volunteered "in mass."[38]

Just as the administration would use bond drives to sell the war, so they would hype the draft.

Registration Day, June 5, 1917, came off like a Super Bowl half-time show. Woodrow Wilson provided an additional motivation to attend by reminding America that any eligible man not showing up, or anyone trying to persuade eligibles not to register, faced a year in prison under the law. By the end of 1917, half a million men had been drafted, in addition to 700,000 who had already volunteered. By war's end, over 24 million men would be registered, but only 2.8 million of them would be drafted.

It is impossible to know how the draft would have fared had the war dragged on into 1919 or 1920, and it would have dragged on had not the German General Staff concluded that the Bolsheviks at home were a greater threat than the doughboys in France. What is clear is that by November 11, 1918, the U.S. government was relying less and less on hype and more and more on hard coercion: prosecutions, work-or-fight orders, and "slacker raids" reminiscent of the Civil War.

No one was drafted after Armistice Day. Troop trains filled with inductees headed for basic training simply turned around and went home. Despite a few postwar pleas and plans for orderly demobilization and the maintenance of a serious force, the army essentially self-destructed. And soon enough, Woodrow Wilson, his mind shattered by a stroke and by the failure of his impossible dream, became to America little more than a fading photo of some old relative, once imposing, now demented and vague.

It is said that the United States turned isolationist, one of many times in our history when periods of war and frenetic activity abroad are followed by withdrawal. This is nonsense. The United States never has been an isolationist nation, certainly not after World War I. A nation that built its population on immigration century after century is not isolationist. A nation that, in the four years of World War I, went from the world's greatest debtor to the world's greatest creditor, could not be isolationist. A nation that, although it refused to join the League of Nations, nevertheless went on a binge of signing and brokering treaties, succoring the affairs of some states, and intervening in the affairs of others, was not isolating itself from the world. When America goes isolationist, it turns away, at least for a while, from itself. It turns away, at least for a while, from that strange and volatile mix of power, idealism, and cynicism that impels us to remake the world in our own image.

Sometimes it's not such a bad idea to turn away. To summarize:

THE FIRST WORLD War, not the Second, provided the template for twentieth-century American military service. It was a complex template. Prior to the war, Progressive social engineers had touted universal military training as a political and social panacea. Training, not war, although some, like Teddy Roosevelt, more than occasionally seemed to prefer combat to other forms of amelioration. When the European war began, the UMT movement segued naturally— and sincerely—into the preparedness movement. Its most ardent proponents may well have been elitists such as Grenville Clark, but they were not hypocrites. When war came, they went.

And when war came, the government chose not to rely on the martial enthusiasms of the people. After the initial wave of volunteering, in August 1917 Congress discontinued further independent recruitment by the services. All would now be processed through the draft, and service would be for the duration. Nearly twenty-four million men registered, but only three million were actually inducted. In theory, this was because manpower was being selected rationally and democratically, through civilian boards with few firm guidelines and enormous powers of discretion. Although by 1918, the slogan was "Work or Fight for All," it was far from clear what those twenty-one million uninducted males were doing. What is clear is that there were endless ways out, from marriage and dependents to putatively vital war work to cashing in those bad teeth or fallen arches or reputation as a strange sort of young man. And many, many institutions, from corporations to professions to universities to small towns and families, benefited from keeping men out. Beneath the alleged national commitment to the war, beneath the "war hysteria," beneath the hype, very quietly, the millions stayed out.

As for preparedness and UMT—after the war, nobody was buying it. But the desire to inculcate the martial virtues and develop young men of character remained. This time, however, the chosen agency of salvation was football.

4

The Real Draft Will Never
Get in the Books

FRANKLIN D. ROOSEVELT DIED on April 12, 1945. He did not live to see the victory. The next day, the *New York Sun* began its list of war dead, a roster that had been appearing every day since December 1941, with the notation, "Roosevelt, F.D. Rank: Commander in Chief." To a nation that had watched the president age and sicken almost week by week toward the end, the tribute seemed apt. Whether you loved him or hated him, and there were few who didn't do one or the other (or both), he had given his life for the cause, as surely as any soldier on a battlefield.

Twenty years or so later, a chant began to be heard on some of America's more prestigious college campuses: "Hey, hey, LBJ, how many kids did you kill today?"

Five years into that chant, a Harvard senior beat the draft. Thirty years after that, a president who as a young man "loathed the military" but flirted with ROTC to maintain his "political viability," left the White House after eight popular years. He was replaced by a man who'd evaded Vietnam service in a rather different way.

The progression from "Roosevelt, F.D., Commander in Chief" to "Hey, hey, LBJ," thence to the presidencies of Bill Clinton and George W. Bush, is a strange and dreary tale. We take here as a kind of spiritual pivot the experience of James Fallows, Harvard 1970. After the war, Mr. Fallows produced one of the most poignant, honest, moving, and enduring articles ever written on the subject of beating the Vietnam draft, "What Did You Do in the Class War, Daddy?"[1]

Fallows drew number 45 in the first draft lottery, held late in 1969 to establish the order of 1970 inductions. As he recounts:

"To answer the call was unthinkable, not only because, in my heart, I was desperately afraid of being killed, but also because, among my friends, it was axiomatic that one should not be 'complicit' in the immoral war effort. Draft resistance, the course chosen by a few noble heroes of the movement, meant going to prison or leaving the country. With much the same intensity with which I wanted to stay alive, I did not want those things either. What I wanted was to go to graduate school, to get married, and to enjoy those bright prospects I had been taught that life owed me."

Fallows did indeed have bright prospects. He would go on to an extraordinary career, from a Rhodes Scholarship to the Carter White House, to decades as a well-regarded journalist and author. But first he and his cohorts had to get through the draft physical. They reported for their physicals.

"There was no mistaking the political temperament of our group. Many of my friends wore red arm bands and stop-the-war buttons. . . . One of the things we had learned from the draft counselors was that disruptive behavior at the examination was a worthwhile political goal, not only because it obstructed the smooth operation of the 'criminal war machine,' but also because it might impress the examiners with our undesirable character traits. . . . Twice I saw students walk up to young orderlies—whose hands were extended to receive the required cup of urine—and throw the vials in the orderlies' faces."

Fallows, a tall, slender man who ran track, hoped to beat the draft by coming in under the minimum allowable weight. His weight that day was 120 pounds, not quite low enough to be safely free with a medical exemption. Then:

"I walked in a trance through the rest of the examination, until the final meeting with the fatherly physician who ruled on marginal cases such as mine. I stood there in socks and underwear, arms wrapped around me in the chilly building. I knew as I looked at the doctor's face that he understood exactly what I was doing.

" 'Have you ever contemplated suicide?' he asked after he finished looking over my chart. My eyes darted up to his. 'Oh, suicide—yes, I've been feeling very unstable and unreliable recently.' He looked at me, staring until I returned my eyes to the ground. He wrote 'unqualified' on my folder, turned on his heel, and left. I was overcome by a wave of relief, which for the first time revealed to me how great my terror had been, and by the beginning of the sense of shame which remains with me to this day.

"It was initially a generalized sense of shame at having gotten away with my deception, but it came into sharper focus later in the day." As the Harvard group was leaving, a bus arrived carrying "the boys from Chelsea, thick, dark-haired young men, the white proles of Boston." Concludes Fallows:

"We knew now who would be killed."

Were he to rewrite this essay today, from the vantage point of middle age, I suspect that he might add something about the ghosts of those who had already been killed, and especially the ghosts of his father's generation. And perhaps, were he aware of "Dick L." and his primal scream that "I HAVEN'T BEEN GIVEN A GOOD ENOUGH REASON" to go to Vietnam, he might consider that a more honest self-justification than all the jargon-laden, invective-laced preening cant about "complicit with the war machine."

It is impossible to understand what happened to American culture in the 1960s without reference to the draft. And it is impossible to understand the draft without repeating: This was an institution that, in war and peace, was designed to keep men out of uniform as well as bring them into it. Ostensibly a rational way to manage manpower in complex economies while preserving basic social values, especially the family, selective service was in fact corrupt by design. It offered not just a modicum of rational management, but a plethora of ways to work, or to abuse, the system. It started in World War I, with the institution of the local board structure. These were given quotas to meet with the tacit understanding that, so long as they were met and the board kept out of the headlines and the courts, no one would look too closely. A complex system of exemptions and deferments was established, often subject to individual interpretation, based upon minimal and sometimes contradictory guidance. A 1960s researcher sat in on the deliberations of one Wisconsin board. What he found was certainly disturbing. Perhaps it was also typical of millions of local board meetings from 1917 to 1973.

> BOARD MEMBER A (looking at a letter): Here's a guy who's working on hydraulic pumps—an engineer. Company says it builds pumps for sewage treatment plants and for drainage systems in missile complexes—therefore, deferment requested because the job of the man is in the national health, safety, and interest.
> BOARD MEMBER B: Sewage plants! Aw, c'mon—the national health?
> BOARD MEMBER A: Hell, how do we know? Maybe our national health is in jeopardy. How do they expect us to know?
> BOARD MEMBER C: Yeah (with sarcasm). Can't let our missiles get wet either—have enough trouble getting them to light as it is.

Forty minutes later, one frustrated man concluded, "If they expect us to decide . . . why in the hell don't they give us something we can make a decision on—something in writing. They tell us one damn thing and then another and it's always 'Headquarters says.'

Let's turn this down and if they don't like it, let Headquarters appeal it."

Later in the meeting:

NEW MEMBER: I'd like to ask a question if I might. We're supposed to decide these cases on the basis of whether deferment is in the national health, safety, or interest?

CHAIRMAN: Yes. That's what the regulations say.

NEW MEMBER: How do we do that?

CHAIRMAN: Well, you get the hang of it after a while. You see, it's sort of like an accordion. Sometimes you stretch it out and get generous with deferments and then other times you squeeze it up tight.

NEW MEMBER: Well, I guess I've got a lot to learn.

And one other case:

BOARD MEMBER A: A deferment to study architecture in graduate school!?

BOARD MEMBER B: Isn't this the rich kid who's given us all the trouble?

CLERK: That's the one.[2]

More often than not, perhaps, that's how it was done. An overworked local board, volunteers, almost entirely white male and heavily veteran, passing judgments as best they could, or as their own prejudices and ideals dictated. Who looked too closely? Certainly not a lot of people during World War II, when passions ran high and the allocation of human beings to military and industrial work, a matter of life and death, was known, generically, as "The Mess in Washington."[3]

In January 1918, fifty-five years after conscription had first been practiced in America, the Supreme Court ruled on its constitutionality. For convenience, the Court consolidated a number of cases into the "Selective Draft Law Cases." Its decision was based upon the kind of logic and rhetoric the Court employs when it knows where it wants to go, but doesn't know how to get there. Their fundamental premise, "As the mind cannot conceive an Army without the men to compose it . . ." was deemed sufficient to rule, unanimously, that the Constitutional distinction between "raising armies" (an eighteenth-century term for hiring professional forces) and "calling forth the militia" (compulsory federal service via the states to deal with invasion, insurrection, and unrest) just didn't matter much anymore. The Court also rejected the contention that conscription constituted involuntary servitude, as prohibited by the Thirteenth Amendment. It did so via an exceptionally arrogant confusion of assertion with proof, and of rhetoric with reality:

"Finally, as we are unable to conceive upon what theory the exaction by government from the citizen of the performance of his supreme and noble duty of contributing to the defense of the rights and honor of the nation, as the result of a war declared by the great representative body of the people, can be said to be the imposition of involuntary servitude in violation of the prohibitions of the Thirteenth Amendment, we are constrained to the conclusion that the contention to that effect is refuted by its mere statement."[4]

And thus the law of the land going into the 1940s: Service is service, no matter how you get there.

Throughout the twenties and thirties, the War Department planned for renewed conscription. They liked the World War I system, especially its practice of drafting "for the duration" and letting the civilians do the dirty work. As a matter of efficiency, they wanted all volunteering to stop when the draft was instituted. This they would get in World War II, though not immediately. After August 1942, men could still apply for the Navy or Marines through their local draft board, but there were no guarantees and, when such volunteers ran short, the other services took unwilling conscripts. The War Department also assumed that there would be no draft until after the next declaration of war, so they did not plan for a truly gargantuan, sudden influx of men.

The Selective Training and Service Act of 1940 took them by surprise.

Although FDR may have concluded that the United States needed to get ready for war as early as 1937, going into 1940 there was no significant popular or political pressure for a draft. Running for an unprecedented third term, FDR certainly wasn't going to propose one. That was done for him, in May 1940, by the private sector, and constitutes one of the most remarkable examples of how civic-minded elites can get things done.[5]

In 1914, when he helped launch the preparedness movement, Grenville Clark was a New York attorney of impeccable breeding, wealth, and quiet access to those who mattered in Washington, D.C. The intervening decades had only solidified his position. His November 1914 letter to fellow Harvard man, former President Theodore Roosevelt, had touted his "little scheme" by adding that "the men in the corps would be men of sufficient means to carry the expenses themselves. . . ."[6] TR, knowing what that meant socially, had responded, "Bully!" and, with Wood's equally ardent backing, it had happened. In the summer of 1915, Clark and 1,200 other "tired businessmen" at Plattsburg formally voted themselves the "First Training Regiment" and later merged with a similar outfit to form the Military Training Camps Association.

Clark went on active duty in 1917 and, to his disgust, spent World War I in D.C. Throughout the interwar years, he cherished his military memories. May 8, 1940 found him at the New York Harvard Club, with eight other men who formed the Executive Committee of the Second Corps Area of the old MTCA. The dinner was a planning event for their upcoming twenty-fifth reunion. Clark pointed out that there was another war on, that the parallels between 1915 and 1940 were ominous, and that it was time to do something. The men at the table agreed.

Clark then sought to apprise his fellow Harvard alum in the White House that a private movement for conscription was under way. His letter to FDR of May 16 informed the president that on May 22 he would be presiding at a private meeting of Plattsburg veterans: "About fifty picked men will be there." After dropping a few names, he stated: "We propose to debate the question of recommending and supporting compulsory military training of a sort suited to our conditions—on the idea that nothing less may suffice to safeguard the U.S." He then noted that, "[a]ssuming that we decide to support such a proposal, the question will arise whether, as a matter of timing, it is opportune to put it forward publicly at this time." Then, after assuring the president that he would have their full support for such measures short of war as he might propose, Clark concluded: "I inform you of this so that if you wish to send me any comment, you may do so."

Roosevelt responded only two days later with a "Dear Grennie" salutation and some subtle gamesmanship and carefully phrased encouragement:

"I see no reason why the group you mention should not advocate military training. . . . I am inclined to think there is very strong public opinion for universal service so that every able-bodied man and woman would fit into his or her place. The difficulty of proposing a concrete set of measures 'short of war' is largely a political one—what one can get from Congress.

"I hope to see you soon."[7]

There is no evidence that FDR put Clark or anyone else up to this. There is every reason to believe that Roosevelt recognized that he'd been sent a political miracle, a way to raise the draft issue without supporting it too soon. He was certainly being disingenuous when he wrote that America desired universal service, male and female. But his response could be taken as encouragement, and his comment on Congress was certainly an invitation to Clark to set his group to working their contacts on Capitol Hill.

This they did, and more. With stately haste, a planning committee was formed, phone calls made, letters written, the National Emergency Committee launched, and conscription demanded.

Congressional sponsors were conveniently found. The War Department, taken almost totally by surprise, was even less thrilled with this civilian initiative than it had been with the 1914 version. The Army's own planning had assumed that conscription would be instituted only after a declaration of war, and it was woefully lacking in trainers and facilities to accommodate a sudden conscript influx. Gradually, the brass, and a not-so-young staff major named Lewis B. Hershey, came around.

It took four months to get both presidential candidates to approve the idea. Isolationist ire notwithstanding, the BurkeWadsworth Bill got through Congress with ease; FDR quickly signed it, then got back to campaigning. It was, all in all, a superb exercise in public participation by the Right People, abetted by the fall of France and the doings at Dunkirk, and accepted by an American people who knew, deep down, that bad things were headed their way.

The bill, mandating one year of active duty within the Western hemisphere only, became law on September 16, 1940. One month later, on October 16, sixteen million men, aged twenty-one to thirty-six, went to election precinct boards to register and be assigned the numbers that would determine their order of induction. The lottery itself took place on October 29. FDR, the War Department, and Major Hershey, who would spend the next three wars and thirty-nine years running the Selective Service System, wanted pomp and historical continuity, a real media event. They used the same fishbowl that had been employed in 1917 to hold 8,994 capsules, each containing one number. The process began under bright lights when Henry L. Stimson, the secretary of war, approached the fishbowl to be blindfolded with a cloth that included a strip cut from one of the chairs used at the signing of the Declaration of Independence. The bowl was periodically stirred with a paddle carved out of a rafter from Independence Hall. Seventeen hours later, Hershey discovered that six capsules had somehow been left out. Always resourceful, he conducted a final minilottery out of a hat.[8] Statistical analysis later showed that the drawing hadn't been entirely random, a result attributed to the way the capsules were loaded and stirred. There was no evidence of tampering. But the drawing was an omen. Making conscription work would be a messy business.

Throughout the war, the government would present the draft as a model of democratic efficiency and equity. "But," writes George Q. Flynn, perhaps the most thorough analyst of America's experience with the draft, "the myth of an egalitarian draft barely survived the passage of the law itself."[9] Once again, Congress had left it to the executive branch to work out the details on deferments and exemptions. These were passed out with joyous prodigality. Over 70 percent of men applying for dependency deferments, citing hardship to their families, got them. Meanwhile the doctors, dentists, and shrinks were flunking people with abandon. Forty percent of registrants washed out at draft board examinations, and another 15 percent at Army exams upon reporting for duty. Nearly a hundred thousand more were rejected for failure to show fourth-grade literacy skills.

In short, of the first two million men examined, half were rejected.[10] Meanwhile, under the law, every student who asked for a deferment to finish his school year, got it. As Flynn wrote: "The draft had been sold as a democratic mechanism. Giving a blanket deferment to those privileged enough to attend college contradicted this idea. Did the nation want laws or regulations that sent the message that 'prior calls shall be made upon the uneducated to defend America.' "[11]

A year later, conscription faced a final legislative challenge. In popular legend, the act needed renewal, and passed by only one vote in the House. This is not correct. The legislation in question extended time of service, including for those already inducted who were approaching the end of their obligated year. Hundreds of thousands of men in uniform felt betrayed, as did their families. But congressional passage and popular acceptance, however grudging, revealed a nation far less than blissfully unaware of danger. It was ugly, but it worked.

And so it went, throughout the war. There would be, of course, major changes and tightenings (and loosenings) as the war proceeded and manpower grew ever more scarce. The myth of fairness would linger. But as Flynn concluded, "From the earliest days of the draft, the rule was special as opposed to equal treatment."[12] The very size of the system—6,443 local boards, 184,000 volunteer members, and a few thousand paid clerks processing hundreds of thousands of items monthly—meant that an awful lot of stuff could get lost, or not get done, as desired. And favored categories could often get what they wanted. These categories varied over time and place. Sometimes it was husbands and fathers. Indeed, according to statistics provided by the Centers for Disease Control, the national birth rate (live births per hundred thousand population) increased from 18.6 in 1940 to 19.5 in 1941 to 21.5 in 1942 to 22.1 in 1943, dropping to 20.5 in 1944 and 19.7 in 1945—after fatherhood deferments had been curtailed. Sometimes it was farm workers or miners or industrial workers. Sometimes it was retail clerks or federal workers. It all depended on chance and circumstance, who you knew, who knew you, and the rest of the human catalog of idealism, vice, and folly. The power of the draft boards was huge, especially because board members were, most emphatically, not average Joes. General Hershey insisted that the members be unpaid, which in practice meant that poor and working men need not apply. The nominating and vetting process ensured that local notables and potentates, all male and save for a couple hundred, all white, would fill the boards. To cross these men, or to question their probity, would be to antagonize the community power structure. No doubt, many of these men, probably most, were honest and sincere. But there is no reason to believe that these "little groups of neighbors" did not contain a percentage who abused their power, or acquiesced to such abuses.

And from the beginning, people knew that it would be so, that many would escape service for one reason or another. General Hershey even laughed at it, or at least tried to get others to laugh. In a 1942 speech at the University of Pennsylvania, Hershey, who had risen from major to major general in two years, read a little poem allegedly written by a draft board clerk. "Clerk's Lament" may not be much as poetry, but it captures the situation very well.

> *Ten little registrants standing in a line;*
> *One joined the Navy, then there were nine.*
> *Nine little registrants sitting on a gate;*
> *One broke a vertebra, then there were eight.*
> *Eight little registrants, talking 'bout Heaven;*
> *One went conscientious, then there were seven.*
> *Seven little registrants, what a strange mix!*
> *One became a pilot, and then there were six.*
> *Six little registrants very much alive;*
> *One went and drowned, and then there were five.*
> *Five little registrants full of canny lore;*
> *One stole a pig, and then there were four.*
> *Four little registrants, spry as they can be;*
> *One became twenty-eight, then there were three.*
> *Three little registrants, all alone and blue;*
> *One fed his relatives, then there were two.*
> *Two little registrants, what can be done!*
> *One went to a psychiatrist, then there was one.*
> *One little registrant to tote a big gun;*
> *He went and got married, and then there were NONE![13]*

And through it all, there was the preinduction equivalent of the million-dollar wound: the IV-F medical exemption. So many men got these that a postwar study could call them "The Lost Divisions." According to this study, eighteen million men were medically examined during the war. About 5.25 million were rejected for medical reasons alone, 970,000 for "emotional disorders" and 716,000 for "mental or educational deficiency."[14] What percentage of these exemptions were legitimate, what percentage faked, what percentage designed to help increase the professional standing of medicine, psychiatry, and psychology, can never be determined.

And again, the role of the medical, psychological, and psychiatric professions, as professions, was pivotal. The military was desperate to minimize problem inductees and was happy to let the shrinks and psychologists zestfully weed them out. General Hershey had wanted psychological and psychiatric screening done at the draft board exams, but there simply weren't enough qualified civilians available. So these tests, mostly five- to fifteen-minute questionnaires and interviews, were conducted at military induction centers by men in uniform who, as a rule, had no prior knowledge of the person. It was mass, superficial, military screening, in direct violation of the spirit of civilian selection, and it was not particularly effective. Despite weeding out as many as 1.85 million men (estimates vary), other millions later developed serious combat and service-related conditions.[15] In the end, concluded John W. Appel, a psychologist who'd done such screening, his own intuition and subsequent studies "determined that that single question, asked at induction, 'Do you want to be in the service?,' predicted actual emotional breakdown better than any other. Negative responses heralded subsequent mental disorder."[16]

A curious reversal of the original "Catch-22"—you can get out if you're insane, but trying to get out only proves your sanity. Still, he may have had a point when he suggested that the worst possible answer, from the mental health perspective, was "When ya gotta go, ya gotta go." Apathy in the face of hardship and danger is rarely benign.

Still, it was the medical doctors who exercised the most power, but for a complex set of reasons. There was no "doctor draft" back then, but one third of the nation's physicians found themselves in uniform. The result was a serious civilian doctor shortage, with serious long-term professional implications. Medicine had only recently attained its exalted status; the last thing the AMA wanted was a national demonstration that non-MDs could do much of their routine work at a fraction of the cost. The fact that this demonstration was under way in the military, as tens of thousands of enlisted medics and corpsmen performed superbly, added an additional incentive to keep their perks—what if all those returning vets demanded socialized medicine? The profession also wanted to maintain a steady stream of male medical students. The negotiations with the government were complex and subtle. The AMA got what it wanted. In return, thousands of civilian doctors donated their services to local boards, where they conducted mostly superficial "screening" examinations . . . and where their decisions usually went unquestioned.[17]

The American people knew all this. And yet, the American people approved. Surveys then and afterward consistently indicated that the American people regarded the system as fair. Why?

One reason might be that so much of the cheating, evasion, and manipulation were done quietly, under the table. Another reason might be that so many people were engaged in the war that it was best not to talk about it at all. But perhaps the most compelling reason, as Paul Fussell, a decorated Army officer who became one of America's great literary scholars, said to me during an interview concerning his book *Wartime*: "That war is a priceless moral resource. People don't want you to mess with it."

Like the war itself, the draft got sanitized, then venerated. In the popular imagination, it set a standard for future wars and future generations. But it was not the right standard. The children of the Greatest Generation would play the same game, but without the discretion or the tact, or the courage, of their elders. In *Wartime*, Fussell noted a common-enough cliché among combat vets: "The real war will never get in the books."[18] Perhaps it might also be said that the real draft never got in the books.

Or did it?

.   .   .

TO WRITE ABOUT the World War II draft is no simple thing. Like so much else of those years, it was chaos, a swirl of ever-changing laws and regulations, procedures and goals. It was mostly improvisation, the management of endless crises, and fatigue. Then there's the matter of all the records that are no longer there, and of all the items that never got written down.

But if the subject itself is chaotic, the notion that the World War II and Vietnam drafts are comparable in their inequities and evasions seems downright obscene. Even the fact that, in both wars, less than half the eligible men served, is hardly comparable. Between 1941 and 1945, sixteen million men and women wore a uniform, out of a population of 130 million, and there was virtual unanimity on the war itself. During the Vietnam era, 1965 to 1973, maybe fifteen million wore a uniform out of a population of 200 million, and there was no unanimity, to say the least. Further, the draft-age pools were far from commensurable: 18–26 (technically, 18–35 if you'd accepted deferment) for Vietnam, 18–44 for World War II. Also—a matter to be considered later—the criteria for conscientious objection were very different during the two periods.

But the fact remains. In both wars, the draft was a complex, diffuse affair that offered, by design, a plethora of ways to beat the system. At one point during the writing of this book, I became concerned about overstating the case, of claiming widespread deliberate draft-dodging when the evidence wouldn't support it. I mentioned this to an e-mail correspondent, Robert Killebrew, a retired army colonel with a distinguished record who has become one of network TV's best military talking heads. Colonel Killebrew replied, "Not surprising, given some of the stories my father told me."

Sadly, those stories are no longer available to the historian. Too many millions of Americans took them to their graves. And yet, there is a remarkable window into the problems and discomforts of that era provided by, of all people, the Selective Service System.

Between 1942 and 1948, SSS published four unclassified reports on their doings and dilemmas. The fact that such sensitive information

would be made public domain in wartime in itself offers a compli-
ment to the American people, in their mature right to know. These
reports aren't slender. They're book-length, with endless statistics
of at least ball-park accuracy and consistency regarding inductions,
deferments, and exemptions. It was for the statistics that I first con-
sulted these volumes. But I quickly became aware that, to understand the era, the prose was far more evocative.

So were the pictures. The first volume, *Selective Service in Peacetime: 1940–41*, featured on page 97 a smiling Brooklyn resident
named Joseph Benito Mussolini above the caption, "He has Serial
No. 1 and is happy." The same volume sternly warned that the new
system was "Not a Missing Persons Bureau" and noted that
"[a]lmost immediately after the [first] registration, hundreds of re-
quests began to pour in on National Headquarters, State Headquarters and local boards for information from wives looking for errant
husbands, creditors for delinquent debtors, girls for lost sweethearts, parents for missing sons—and some citizens were looking
for men whom they believed should be brought to the bar of justice,
not infrequently through a motive of pure revenge."[19]

The second volume, *Selective Service in Wartime: 1941–42*, showed
another happy registrant who'd turned in a local clerk who'd demanded a fifty-dollar bribe. He was happily receiving the congratu-
lations of the Pennsylvania State Commissioner. "Dishonesty," the
caption noted, "has been very rare."[20] That type of blatant dishonesty, no doubt. The third report, *Selective Service as the Tide of War
Turns: 1943–44*, after fatherhood deferments had been curtailed,
showed two more happy men, and their families. "A saxophonist
with a family of seven. He has passed the preinduction physical examination and is ready for induction." And a "Thirty-four-year-old
father of ten is called for induction February 3, 1944." This volume
also featured two unhappy people, a "registrant, aged 28, [who] declared Mary Ann Sheridan as his dependent. Mary Ann Sheridan was
a horse. His claim for dependency kept him out of the Army for two
years." Another, an unnamed female "clerk of Yonkers, N.Y., spirited

away her sweetheart's file and destroyed the file of her brother-in-law."[21]

The final volume, *Selective Service and Victory: 1944–45*, featured a "Wisconsin youth of 19" who demanded "draft exemption as hereditary 'chieftain' of Menominee Indians and descendant of 'lost' Potowatomi tribe, basing his exemption on treaties with the United States Government. The judge gave him 10 days to register with his draft board." Also featured was an unnamed man in uniform, "wearing the ETO ribbon with 3 battle stars, the combat infantryman's badge, and the good conduct medal." He'd enlisted at age fourteen in 1941 and "was required to register after separation upon becoming 18." Holding his registration papers, he did not look particularly happy.[22]

Most of the text of these reports is devoted to explanations of regulations and procedures, plus changes and changes to the changes. But occasionally, in the dry yet subtle language of government, acknowledgment of inequity comes through.

The first report set the tone, conceding two major items. The first was that keeping men out of uniform was also a major objective, one that SSS would discharge according to its own view of things. Fill the ranks, yes. "However, if Selective Service were restricted to this objective only, its task would be simple, but such a restriction of function would wreck the social, religious, political, and industrial life of the Nation. . . . we insist that there be a minimum of disturbance to the national life consistent with the current needs."[23] Since all disturbance, like all politics, is local, boards were authorized, in effect, to err on the side of stability, especially in preserving families.

But the boards had structural problems of their own. Ideally, boards would contain roughly the same number of registrants, about 3,500 men. But since the law required at least one board per county, many had very small numbers. Others were far in excess of the goal. Local quotas were supposed to be determined solely by each board's inventory of I-A, available for unlimited duty, registrants, but it

didn't always work that way. Boards under pressure to meet their
quotas might tighten up on deferments and exemptions that other
boards would grant routinely. The on-again/off-again nature of
the "available for limited service" category (sometimes I–B, sometimes I–L) complicated things. The Army finally nixed this category entirely in 1944, on the grounds that they had enough men
already in uniform—the sick, wounded, and recovering—who could
perform limited duties. And it was in 1944, as combat intensified
and the manpower pool drained, that medical exemptions skyrock-
eted, that the Army loosened the rules against taking petty and
sometimes not so petty convicted criminals who had finished their
sentences.

And how could a state assign full quotas to local boards in areas
already denuded of young men—or areas that had already produced
more than their share of Gold Star mothers? How often, one must
wonder, did local examining physicians or local boards decide that
protecting their remaining young men now took precedence over
the war? Towns and counties, like individuals, could reach their
limit.

Over and over, the reports confessed to inequities, at one point
stating explicitly, in regard to occupational deferments:

"Furthermore, there is the human element to consider. This element always enters into all judicial problems. Honest men have
differences of opinion. Some have training and background which
fits them to understand the problems of industry, while others in
their patriotic zeal wish to see all the men of their community who
do not have dependency deferments, put in the armed forces."[24]

The "human element," indeed.

The human element also entered into the handling of minorities. Japanese Americans were, as the third report put it, "Not acceptable for service temporarily" and anyway, local boards reported
"lack of current addresses" for many, noting their "compulsory removal . . . to War Relocation Authority projects located farther in-
land." Starting in 1943, Japanese American men were permitted to

volunteer. Local boards were instructed to determine whether these men were physically qualified and "otherwise acceptable."[25]

African Americans posed a greater problem. The law specified that induction be totally nondiscriminatory, but the services insisted on submitting quotas, small quotas, for colored troops. The reports show a strained neutrality on the matter, sometimes suggesting that proper use is not being made of these men, at other times pondering the high rate of rejection for reasons ranging from illiteracy to venereal disease. But since neither General Hershey nor General Marshall nor FDR was willing to make a wartime issue out of it, justice would have to wait.

One of the great slogans of World War II was, "This time let's finish the job." The day after the job was finished in Europe, May 9, 1945, President Truman signed Public Law 54, extending the draft for one year. The job still needed finishing in the Pacific and, it was already becoming clear, a few more decades of vigilance awaited. However, political pressures proved insurmountable. The American military basically discharged itself; the draft ended on October 31, 1946. At some visceral level, President Truman favored universal military training, but never plumped too hard for it. Other Americans, including General Marshall, did, or at least said they did. Some wanted national service with military and nonmilitary options. You can read their writings from the 1945–48 period, change a few dates and names, and still use it today. Sometimes recycling works. However, after ten years of depression and nearly five years of war, few Americans were interested in going on crusades either foreign or domestic. There was also The Bomb to pretend to depend upon.

In 1945, the War Department authorized a Selective Service Medal for those who'd spent the war sending others to war, or keeping others out of war. At first, it seemed that all the SSS had to do was wrap up its affairs, destroy its files, accept its medals, and fade away quietly. However, due to Cold War pressures and postwar military manpower shortfalls, Congress enacted the Selective Service Act of 1948. It was basically the World War II system, minus the goal/pretense of allocating manpower to meet wartime needs. To borrow a line from a famous folk song, it took what it needed and left the rest. General Hershey kept his job as director. The laughably misnamed Universal Military Training and Service Act of 1951, pushed through Congress in part because America was pissed that so many World War II vets had been recalled for Korea, established the final system. A million and a half men were drafted for that war. Another million and a half eligibles were not, while over 600,000 World War II vets were recalled. And it was clear that Selective Service was back in its old saddle when General Hershey lamented in 1951: "What I have to do is figure out how to raise an armed force of 3,500,000 without taking anybody."[26]

5

Resistance Is Not Futile

TO THE GENERATION THAT CAME of military age during the fifties and Vietnam, General Lewis B. Hershey was an old man who had never been young. I recall my own amazement at seeing a picture of him as a major: not at all a bad-looking guy back then. But that was back then. In his old age, he became to millions of young Americans evil personified, and to millions of others, little more than—what was that term of damnation back then?—*irrelevant.*

Historian George Flynn, a man who devoted his academic life to studying the draft, began his biography of General Hershey with a tale of the old man giving a speech at Berkeley in 1970. Out of uniform, the seventy-seven-year-old seemed, in Flynn's phrase, "like a refugee from a park bench." The title of his presentation: "Age Talks with Youth."

Hershey got heckled even before he started. He tried a few

jokes, but the crowd in its righteousness didn't care to respond. When one student called out an obscenity, Hershey replied, "I'll probably regret the part that I've had . . . to keep this boy in college." When another asked how he felt about killing so many people, he replied that "this is flattery that I simply can't stand." When he finally lashed out with the one fact that the students couldn't bear to have stated, that "some people who are taking all the benefits won't keep their mouths shut," the audience response became predictable. One student summed it all up by telling him:

"I'd like to—uh—like I'm thinking and I'm looking at you, and like you're death personified. . . . Like I don't want to talk to you because you're in the past, and we're here, and we're now, and we're alive. . . . You're a good German. . . . Everybody here is so mad at you, that if they saw you on the street and didn't have just respect for your age, and knowing that things are just going to happen naturally, they'd rip you off . . . and I think I'm rational, I kinda have pity, because you can't make sense of what I'm saying right now, but like people here make sense."[1]

It would be easy here to focus on this one student's half-assed hissy fit, and on the fact that Hershey had committed an unforgivable breach of campus decorum. He'd mentioned the hard truth that his tormentors were not those who'd suffered from his ministrations. But perhaps General Hershey's state of mind might be more, as they said back then, relevant. According to Flynn, Hershey responded to the tirade with a mumbled, "Some sense." No doubt, at the end of his long, perhaps overlong, career, he felt bewildered and betrayed. Perhaps he looked back to the halcyon days of World War II, when everybody did his part and nobody worked the system to stay out . . .

But he couldn't have. That was not the way it was. And he knew it, for he'd presided over a system that let millions of young and not-so-young men avoid service legally. The statistics would never reveal who got the favors and the benefits of the doubt, any more than it would reveal which VIPs had made phone calls on whose behalf, or whose records had disappeared, or what actions just never got around to being taken. Those statistics never existed. But the man who signed those four reports knew that, by the millions, such things had happened. A careful reading of those reports indicate that a lot of people knew, and that, throughout the war, there had been protests and outcries and commissions and investigations and remedial actions and the rest. But it never became a serious national scandal. Why not?

Because there was a war on. And the vast majority of the American people were simply too committed to that effort to be distracted by the matter of legal evasions. It was no doubt hard for one family with a son or sons at war to see another family's sons walk free. But in the myriad ways that a cohesive society has of quietly and privately dealing with such problems, they were dealt with.

And after the war, if you'd managed to evade service, you shut up about it.

So in the end, General Hershey's hands were not clean. For he had presided over a system that, in good American tradition, offered plenty of ways out. Hershey, who had served in France in World War I but never saw combat, was no killer. Nor was he a "good German"—a phrase properly recast as "good Nazi." And perhaps it was the tragedy of his life, and a tragedy of his nation, that it was this business of keeping young men out of uniform that finally undid him.

The Korean War ended in 1953. The draft did not. And the great peacetime game began for millions of men whose goal was to get out completely via a IV-F medical exemption, or else to string enough deferments together to make it to age twenty-six, when for practical purposes, liability ceased. II-S, the now-standard college- and grad-student deferment, was there for the asking. III-A, registrant with a child living with him or deferred because of hardship to dependents, could also work. II-A, deferral because of civilian agricultural employment, was available for those who liked to farm. IV-D was for minister of religion or divinity student for the spiritually inclined; your ministry didn't always have to be full-time. Less desirable, but open to those who couldn't quite make it to IV-F was I-Y, available for service only in time of war or national emergency. Best of all was V-A, registrant over the age of liability.

Between Korea and Vietnam, the draft was an accepted part of American life, accepted in the same manner as the IRS. You didn't love it, but you acknowledged its necessity and enjoyed hearing jokes about it on that newest of intellectual genres, the late-night television show. The draft's demands were not onerous. During the years from 1955 to 1964, Selective Service never took more than 152,000 men per year; most calls ranged from 80,000 to 120,000, depending on world events and who wanted to make an impression on whom.[2] Nor was military service any kind of political litmus test, liberal or conservative. Personal and family considerations usually determined attitude and not a few men, such as Norman Podhoretz, were happy to be drafted because it relieved them of the necessity of explaining to their parents why they wanted the experience. Many men didn't, but those such as Dick Cheney, who had "other priorities" during their eligible years, were hardly hypocrites.

Some people fretted over how many young men were failing their physical and mental exams, but that was typical of the fifties. Back then, the "Silent Generation" was also known as the "Wasted Generation"—too fat, too dumb, too happy. George Walton, a retired Army colonel who'd worked in the Selective Service System, wrote: "Flabby, obese, or illiterate, the rejectees are usually chronically unemployed or future recipients of our welfare doles." He was also furious when President John Kennedy reinstated marriage as reason for deferment in 1963, but conceded that "[I]f there was to be any pretense of universality in the Universal Military Training Act, the numbers of those available for military service had to be sharply reduced. The exclusion of married men was a quick and easy way to drain off the pool." Walton was also exercised about the decline in national morals, civility, and responsibility. The Army, he felt, could sure improve the "empty heads and wasted bodies" that now characterized American youth.

The Wasted Generation, jeremiad to those hideous fifties, is a wonderful book, a breath of fresh fumes. It ought to be reissued.[3]

In many ways, Walton was not wrong. Between July 1950 and June 1965, nearly *half* of all men called to induction flunked their physical or mental requirements, over three million, all told.[4] And youth was a subject of growing national concern. Still, despite, or perhaps because of, Walton and a few million like him, America was happy with the draft arrangement. And General Hershey clearly enjoyed his status as one of Washington, D.C.'s irreplaceable, or perhaps merely impossible to get rid of, elders. Along with FBI director J. Edgar Hoover and nuclear submarine maven Hyman Rickover, who had their own ways of assuring long tenure, Hershey was a fixture, and proud of it.[5] Indeed, in many ways, Hershey and Rickover were bureaucratic soul mates. Both were career officers who faced dead ends after World War II. Both remained on active duty for decades more, in niches they had created. They assured their tenure by knowing more about their respective subjects than anyone else, and by cultivating relations with Congress. And both stayed on so long that they had to be fired.

Admiral Rickover regarded the nuclear submarine program as both his personal property and his personal gift to the United States. General Hershey took a similar proprietary attitude toward Selective Service. And as the baby boom began approaching military age, it became clear that there would soon be a vast excess of bodies over peacetime requirements. So Hershey got into social engineering. By the sixties, he was taking credit not just for keeping the Army's boots filled, but changing America permanently, and for the better. The policy was called "Channeling," and should not be confused with communicating with the dead. Or maybe it should. Wrote Jean Carper in 1967:

"Time has left Selective Service untouched. A visit to the Selective Service headquarters at 1724 F Street, Washington, D.C., is like returning to the age of Dickens. In the six-story gray building and its brick annex across the street you can find aging men bent over ill-lit desks, surrounded by old wooden filing cabinets. Painstakingly, by hand, they record figure after figure on large yellow ledger sheets that cover their desk tops and hang over onto the floor. These men are keeping track of our 33 million draft registrants with *pencil and paper*. General Hershey does not allow computers; he does not believe in them. (He does allow adding machines, I am told, although I did not see any.)"[6]

Most local boards were not as well equipped or staffed. But they were adequate enough for the work described in Government Printing Office publication number 899.125, first issued in 1965—just as the whole program was about to blow up in their faces.[7]

"One of the major products of the Selective Service classification process," the item began, "is the channeling of manpower into many endeavors, occupations, and activities that are in the national interest." It was no longer the war effort: There was no war. It was now "the national interest." Noting that "More than ten years ago it became evident that something additional had to be done," the publication went on:

"While the best-known purpose of Selective Service is to procure manpower for the armed forces, a variety of related processes take place outside delivery of manpower to the active armed forces. Many of these may be put under the heading of 'channeling manpower.' Many young men would not have pursued a higher education if there had not been a program of student deferment. Many young scientists, engineers, tool and die makers, and other possessors of scarce skills would not remain in their jobs in the defense effort if it were not for a program of occupational deferments. Even though the salary of a teacher has historically been meager, many young men remain in that job, seeking the reward of a deferment. The process of channeling manpower by deferment is entitled to much credit for the large number of graduate students in technical fields and for the fact that there is not a greater shortage of teachers, engineers, and other scientists. . . ."

The publication goes on to assert that, absent universal military training or service, the sound young American male is pressured and encouraged to make choices beneficial to himself and his country. Meanwhile, "[i]n the less patriotic and more selfish individual, it [the draft] engenders a sense of fear, uncertainty, and dissatisfaction which motivates him, nevertheless, in the same direction. He complains of the uncertainty which he must endure; he would like to be able to do as he pleases; he would appreciate a certain future with no prospect of military service or civilian contribution, but he complies with the needs of the national health, safety, or interest—or is denied deferment."

Channeling, the publication concluded, is nothing other than "[t]he device of pressurized guidance . . . the American or indirect way of achieving what is done by direction in foreign countries where choice is not permitted. . . . Some accept the alternatives gladly—some with reluctance. The consequence is approximately the same."

In peacetime, perhaps. But as another adage of the 1940s had it, "Don't you know there's a war on?"

DRAFT RESISTANCE WAS not, of course, an invention of the baby boomers. It was always there. The Civil War draft defused much of it, except for an occasional riot, by permitting virtually automatic avoidance, at least for those who could raise the money. World War I wasn't quite that simple. According to Flynn, somewhere between 350,000 and 2 million men (a rather large "somewhere") failed to register. By war's end, over 337,000 had been officially charged with "desertion" from the draft. World War II was different. Over 300,000 violations were referred to the FBI; nearly 12,000 violators were sent to prison.[8] During Vietnam, as noted, only 3,250 men went to prison for all draft-related violations. Also during Vietnam, according to President Ford's clemency commission, of the 15,980,000 men who never served, 570,000 were classed as real or apparent violators. About 209,000 were accused but only 8,750 were convicted.[9] The pattern of resisting the draft established in the 1860s thus held into the 1960s: much sound and fury during the war, then forgetting it ever happened.

Still, there was something different about the resistance, if such it was, of the 1960s. In a sense, "resistance" is like a declaration of war. It doesn't oblige you to do anything in particular. As Michael S. Foley, a sympathetic historian, discovered in his study of the Harvard "We Won't Go" movement, signing the statement "did not commit the signers to action or even a clearly defined strategy of resistance. 'Our policy is open,' admitted one spokesman for the group."[10] Other groups, such as the probably (and sadly) apocryphal Committee for Violent Non-Action, adopted other strategies. But by and large, it was a matter of individual discretion. And few would question your decision, provided your heart and your politics were in the right place.

When teaching "War and Society" courses at Georgetown University in the 1980s, I liked to present my students with a question. Why did so much of the so-called resistance assume the form it did: a carnival superimposed on a tragedy? To get at the answer, I would then do an exercise borrowed from Harry Summers's analysis of the war, *On Strategy*.

Treat Vietnam, I would tell my students, as a war college exercise. What do you have to do to win? The answer is obvious. First, seal off the country by moving the borders outward, permanently outward, into Laos, Cambodia, and North Vietnam. Blockade North Vietnam. Use airpower massively against meaningful targets. Then help the South Vietnamese to deal with the insurgency in their own way. None of this happened at the start, although we did just about all of it on our way out. What did happen, once it became apparent that victory was not seriously sought, was that other agendas took over: political, budgetary, military, technological. Things that made no sense along the banks of the Mekong could make a great deal of sense along the banks of the Potomac.

Now, envision the "War at Home" as a kind of antiuniverse. If you want to stop a war—if it's clear that the president won't quit and Congress won't cut off funds and the Supreme Court's too busy ruling on prisoners' rights and pornography—what do you do? The "war college answer" is clear. All those young men seriously opposed to the war should have turned in their II-S student deferments, demanded accelerated induction, then shown up on the appointed day and refused to take that one step forward. Legally, you cannot be inducted without your consent, and at the ceremony, you signify that consent by taking one step forward. Your first act as a service person is then to take the oath.

We know that military victory in Vietnam was never seriously sought and, even when militarily attained, proved impossible to convert into political victory. But what might have happened if ten or a hundred thousand young men had taken this course of action, in solidarity with and in memory of their brothers who had gone to war? How long could the war have gone on with the prisons overflowing?

We'll never know. What we do know is that it didn't happen, that drugs and riot and music and sex ("Girls say yes to guys who say no") became the preferred style of resistance, plus occasional forays into more perilous realms that ended rather abruptly after Kent State. Why?

Again, we can skip the amateur psychoanalysis. Suffice it to point out that people need to feel right about themselves. Not just good. Right. In order to achieve this feeling of rightness, millions of draft-age men and women constructed elaborate cathedrals of justification that remain, to this day, as precious and unquestionable as World War II was for its participants. Jim Fallows got it right. All the fancy mental gymnastics and gyrations, all the self-serving pronouncements, fell silent when he looked into the faces of the Chelsea boys, they who would die. Another Harvard boy who went on to a fine career as a writer also got it right.

Today, Mark Helprin is that rarest of cultural commodities, a brilliant and bestselling novelist of politically conservative beliefs. He is also a frequent contributor to the *Wall Street Journal* and other serious publications, and an ardent supporter of the Iraq war. In 1992, he spoke at West Point.

"If I were Bill Clinton I would take 10,000 words to explain this and say nothing, but I'm not Bill Clinton and I can get to the heart of it in eight: What I did was called dodging the draft."[11]

It is important to be clear here about what Helprin is and is not saying. By the standards of the U.S. Army, he was legitimately medically unfit for service by virtue of his eyes. This provided him with the equivalent of the "Million-Dollar Wound." And therefore he would not have to participate in a war he considered unnecessary, unwise, and unjust. But the fact of his disqualification robbed him of his own moral responsibility to take a stand against the war. Many years ago, I asked Jim Fallows what he would have done in 1970, from a more mature perspective. He told me that he wished he'd passed his physical and then refused induction. I recall having a similar conversation with Mark Helprin in the early '90s. I don't remember his exact response, but I believe it was the same. Perhaps he could have gotten a medical waiver because of his eyes, or faked the test, or got the examining physician to lie. I don't know. But I do sense that Helprin's unease transcends Vietnam and its ambiguous legacy. He abandoned his native land in its time of need. Yes, in his scheme of things, it was honorable to serve in the Israeli army. But that honor was insufficient to negate the dishonor of what, to him, was draft-dodging *legitimized by the system*.

Helprin's greatest self-indictment proved the same as Fallows's. He was not with his people when he should have been. "For that I was not with you," he told the cadets, "in my time, at Khe Sanh and Danang and Hue, and all the other places, is for me now, looking back, a great surprise, an even greater disappointment, and a regret that I will carry to my grave."

Millions of other men, apparently, feel the same way. The

"Stolen Valor" phenomenon—men, often men of considerable attainment, posing as Vietnam veterans—has occasioned much comment and embarrassment over the years. So has the Census Bureau's revelation that, if you believe all the claims, over thirteen million *living* Americans served in Vietnam, about ten million more than the total. And so has the discovery that Vietnam was in no way a poor man's war. It was middle class, broadly defined, from the start almost until the end.[12]

In sum, there have turned out to be two kinds of haunting after Vietnam: that of those who served, and that of those who did what they did to stay out, then packaged it as a higher moral probity, then realized that both actions were wrong. The pretense has, over the past few decades, evolved into a style that, as Kathy Roth-Douquet and Frank Schaeffer point out, makes reasoned dialogue for and against the Iraq war and about military ever harder to attain. It is a style that has been passed down to succeeding generations.

But what of those, then and now, who do not find "my country right or wrong" sufficiently compelling? Or "I should have been there with them" sufficiently primal? According to the Ford Commission, 171,700 were awarded the status of "conscientious objector." Of those, 75,500 were not certified as having completed their term of alternative service. Of these, 29,300 never got called, due to high lottery numbers. Of the rest, 1,200 went to prison. The rest, 45,000, walked away.

Conscientious objection, pacifism, and nonviolence are not the same things. Nonviolence may be a personal commitment or a political tactic. Pacifism is a kind of foreign policy. Conscientious objection denotes considered refusal to participate in war, or at least some kinds of war, on deeply held religious or moral grounds. At one level, the issue of conscientious objection arises only in relation to conscription. In a volunteer situation, if you don't want to serve, you don't join. But it's not as simple as that.

. . .

THE UNITED STATES has made provision for conscientious objectors, at least on parchment, since before there was a United States.
On July 18, 1775, in a resolution urging the states to form mass
militias, the Continental Congress noted: "As there are people who,
from religious principles, cannot bear arms in any case, this Congress intend no violence to their consciences, but earnestly recom-
mend it to them, to contribute liberally in this time of universal
calamity, to the relief of their distressed brethren in the several
colonies, and to do all other services to their oppressed Country,
which they can consistently with their religious principles. . . ."[13]
After independence, several states included similar language in their
own constitutions. Early versions of the Second Amendment contained explicit language securing the right of conscientious objection. Apparently, these were stricken due to fear that the federal
government might abuse groups and individuals by declaring them
conscientious objectors and disarming them.

From the beginning, the formula was clear. An objector did not
have to be personally nonviolent. He did have to be a total spiritual
pacifist, opposed to all warfare, based upon religious belief, in this
case, Christian belief. The vast majority of objectors were members
of what came to be known as "well-recognized peace sects"—
Quakers, Brethren, and such. This formula held throughout the
nineteenth century, although how often it was honored in practice
remains difficult to tell. The literature of American pacifism is filled
with tales of men imprisoned, beaten, and worse for failure to show
up for militia drill, or to get their heads sufficiently wrapped around
the Union or Confederate causes.[14]

The World War I situation was complex. By executive order,
Wilson extended this status to non-members of traditional peace
sects who were nonetheless, by reason of "religious training and belief," opposed to participation in war. So, you could not be made to
fight. However, back then, you *could* be drafted against your will.
This meant, among other things, you found yourself in the hands of

the military, not the civilian justice systems. During that war, 57,000 men were certified as conscientious objectors. Of the 30,000 who then passed their physical and mental tests, 21,000 were inducted. What happened to them afterward wasn't always pretty.

Walter Guest Kellogg was an army major in the judge advocate division. He served as chairman of the Board of Inquiry, whose task it was to travel the country and rule on the status of objectors in uniform. Some might be assigned to civilian work, others discharged, others imprisoned. It all depended on the board and the impression the individual made. Kellogg formed some definite opinions of this group. In his 1919 book, *The Conscientious Objector*, he divided them into three groups: the sect member; the independent, idealistic religious objector; and the secular objector, usually a socialist. To Kellogg, the sect member:

"Views life through extremely narrow lenses. . . . He knows nothing of what is going on in the world. . . . One feels there is something definitely wrong with this boy. He presents an ignorance that is astounding. . . . Stupid and dull as his mind, such as it is, is, it is definitely made up."[15]

The idealistic objector, Kellogg went on, is equally religious but personally very different from the sect member. "The first class was entirely lacking in social vision; this man has entirely too much of it. . . . the frailties of human beings, and even their wars, are things to be dealt with only through gentleness and love. He is impracticable and visionary; his mentality is only half-baked. . . . This country was not their country—they were only here temporarily as 'ambassadors of Christ.' "[16]

As for the third type, the well-educated socialist or radical: "Much may be overlooked in an ignoramus; much may be excused in a moron; but much, surely, can with reason be expected in a man of intelligence . . . one who has had all the advantages which birth, environment and education can give. . . . He is egotistical and self-centered. He argues forcibly the cause of 'Me against the

Universe.' . . . Many of them are simply 'nuts,' as they are called in
the camps; some have had little or no education; some have had too
much."[17]

The same types would appear, again and again, through to
Vietnam.

Those of us who have known genuine conscientious objectors
have often found them to be admirable people, serious and disciplined, even if we don't share their views. But many, too many, have
also been connivers and manipulators, such as the World War I objector who calculated: "I'd rather get thirty years, like [name omit-
ted] than fifteen. . . . and I don't want five years—a man *might* have
to serve that!"[18] Some came to resent the uses to which their sincerity was put. J. K. Osborne, one of the few who went to prison as a
draft resister during Vietnam, once described his sense of a rally at
which he was a guest of honor. One man, bragging from the podium
of his organizing efforts, "reeked of self-importance. . . . The
woman [speaker] bore out my doubts. Everything she said that afternoon she had found elsewhere. Her mannerisms on the platform
she took from Hitler. Her rhetoric she took from Norman Mailer.
Her logic from—well, the best I can describe it is 1950s coffee-
house. . . . The whole rally had made no sense. No sense! Suddenly
I feared. I was chilled. I wondered how many of those at the rally,
the young people, would next year, or the year after, be part of the
mass of indifference which they were today supposedly rebelling
against? . . . I very nearly went down to enlist in the Coast Guard."[19]

Perhaps the most that can be said of those who took the conscientious objector route, in whatever war, is that a CO exemption is a
lot like a medal. Only the man who wears it really knows what it's
worth.

World War II codified the principle that any man conscien-
tiously opposed to war by reason of religious training and belief was
eligible to perform uniformed noncombatant service (often as
medics who showed incredible courage) or alternative civilian service. Those absolutists who refused all service might go to prison,

but at least it would be a civilian prison. One group did. The Jehovah's Witnesses were not qualified for exemption because, even though they opposed all secular war, they would fight in divinely mandated holy wars. Their endurance and cohesion in prison became the stuff of legend. And there matters stood until 1965.[20]

It was in the *Seeger* decision that the Supreme Court opened the possibility of exemption to everybody. Now, CO status could be granted, without an affiliation in any denomination, nor even a belief in God. Mr. Seeger "preferred to leave the question as to his belief in a Supreme Being open," but held that his skepticism or disbelief in the existence of God did "not necessarily mean lack of faith in anything whatsoever." He did claim "belief in and devotion to goodness and virtue for their own sakes."

The Court honored his request. The vital passage from the decision reads:

"The test of religious belief within the meaning of the exemption . . . is whether it is a sincere and meaningful belief occupying in the life of its possessor a place parallel to that filled by the God of those admittedly qualified for the exemption. . . . Local boards and courts are to decide whether the objector's beliefs are sincerely held and whether they are, in his own scheme of things, religious; they are not to require proof of the religious doctrines nor are they to reject beliefs because they are not comprehensible."[21]

In effect, the Court changed the standard from the theological to the psychological. Most anything might serve, provided it opposed participation in all war and was held with sufficient sincerity. Christian, Buddhist, Spinoza, Kant, Gandhi, something encountered once on a men's room wall, or perhaps religious intense veneration for Muhammad Ali's "I ain't got no quarrel with them Viet Cong"—whatever works for you. True, the Court ruled that beliefs must not be merely intellectual, derived from mere knowledge and reason. But five years later, in the *Welsh* case, the Court ruled that even someone whose beliefs did not fit the *Seeger* criteria could be eligible, provided the Court's definition took precedence over the objector's. In another case, *Gillette*, the Court ruled against so-called selective conscientious objection: picking and choosing your wars. While one might rate CO exemption by virtue of some exceptionally impressive hallucination, opposition to some wars, however based, was a nonstarter.

And there the law stands, regarding the legal rights of those who may seek to be excused from future wars. All or nothing. All, for those who can demonstrate sincerity in their total opposition. Nothing for those who might do the hard work of making real-world judgments about specific real-world wars and possible wars.

Insane, perhaps. But if there is to be any renewal of citizen service in this country, this is the basis from which it must proceed. Not from patriotism or from philosophies of citizenship and consent, but from a new understanding of objection—the kind of objection codified in the cry, "I haven't been given a good enough reason." That's what the rest of this book is about.

But first, a few words concerning a group of human beings who have, so far, been almost totally ignored in this matter of military service and its meanings.

6

The Woman Question

WOMEN NOW COMPRISE 15 percent of our total military force, a percentage that can only increase. Over 143,000 have gone to war since 9/11, providing a database of female military performance such as has never existed before. Women now routinely go into combat, or have combat come to them, in Iraq and Afghanistan as pilots and flight crews, as support troops doing base and convoy protection, as military police taking on infantry tasks, and as individuals attached (for the present, illegally) to small combat units and special operations forces. They go as medics, communicators, intel types, and to handle Muslim women and children.

None of the predicted disasters have occurred. Forget for a moment what made the headlines, Jessica Lynch and the ill-trained, ill-led, and ill-fated 507th Maintenance Company. Forget also for a moment Lynndie England and the Abu Ghraib Film Festival. Forget also General Janis Karpinski's well-compensated whining that she was made the sacrificial lamb because she was a woman. These travesties and tragedies derived from far greater problems than the presence of women. They were failures of leadership, training, discipline, and morality at many levels. The fact is, as of this writing, there have been no significant combat failures due to the presence of women. There has been no epidemic of pregnancies. There have been no massive breakdowns in unit discipline or cohesion. Had there been, somebody would have leaked it by now, especially to a religious and cultural right that sees women in combat as a potential hot-button issue. "Use the war to take back the culture," I once heard one of them say. Welcome to Culture War II.

Still, like Japanese soldiers holed up in their caves, these Americans are unable to admit that the war over women at war is over. Five years of hard experience indicates that there are no remaining reasons to bar women from full equality under arms, no deficiencies (including physical conditioning) that cannot be corrected. Further, there is every reason to believe that this issue can help American women, and their men, recover from those long, ugly decades during which feminism devolved into an exercise in man-hating petulance, self-obsesssion, and mindless antimilitary bigotry.

I had personally made peace with a certain moral dissonance. I believed in equality, the equality of men and women who share the world, and are responsible for it, together. But in politics, who does things can matter as much as what gets done. Like millions of other men, I had no problem with items such as the Equal Rights Amendment. But damned if I was going to give it to *them*. As for women in the military: I'd known and served with a few, respected them mostly, and was appalled at the feminist assault on the institution, the scandals they manipulated, and the excesses they generated. I'd done a few articles on these matters and had considerable sympathy for Elaine Donnelly, president of the Center for Military Readiness, when she got hit with a potentially bankrupting feminist SLAPP: Strategic Lawsuit Against Public Participation. Elaine, who has spent decades trying to limit women's military roles, had been publicizing leaked reports of Navy and Air Force relaxation of standards for female flight candidates and pilots. Lawyers for navy Lieutenant Carey Dunai Lohrenz accused Elaine and one hundred "John Does" to be named later of, among other things, ruining her self-confidence as a fighter pilot. (Where is Tom Cruise when you really need him?) After several years, the suit was dismissed. Lohrenz, having finally been judged an inadequate combat pilot, was reassigned to fly VIP jets. I never did find out if I was among the hundred culpable males who'd written on the subject. Afterward, I lost interest in the whole issue. In 2004, I got interested again.

Women have always been involved in war. Since the beginning, they have been involved as victims. That old Roman adage, *Vae victis*, woe to the vanquished, has always held a special meaning for the women of the losing side. Women have also been involved as "camp followers," a phrase that should never be taken to mean only "prostitutes." Well into the nineteenth century, women routinely accompanied armies, officially and unofficially, as wives, mothers, cooks, seamstresses, nurses, and in many other capacities. The all-male military, living in monastic barracks and self-sustaining, is an ideal (rarely achieved) of the seventeenth- and eighteenth-century Western professionalization of war, and not the historical norm.

Women have also fought, although if the male historical record is to be believed, usually only *in extremis*. From the Old Testament's Deborah to Joan of Arc to Vietnam's Trung sisters to the women's regiments of the Soviet Union during their Great Patriotic War, women have borne arms, and well. Most often, after hostilities ceased or the immediate peril passed, so did their participation. Only one nation, Israel, has routinely drafted women and (popular myth notwithstanding) has not utilized them as combatants, equal to men, as a matter of policy. (This is changing slowly.)

The United States has never drafted women, although the idea was kicked around a bit during World War II. Nor does the United States currently require women to register for the draft. As a rule, in these matters, the Supreme and lesser courts have deferred to the legislative branch, which in turn defers to the military's estimate of its own requirements. The Defense Department's estimate has traditionally been that women should not be drafted because it would be unnecessary, disruptive, and counterproductive. Such is their stance today.

However, since 9/11, the Defense Department has embarked on a historically unprecedented experiment. Over 147,000 American women have participated in the Iraq and Afghan wars as volunteer professionals and, increasingly, as combatants. We now have a database the likes of which has never existed before and this database reveals three things: First, the American military is now irrevocably dependent upon women. Second, it is time to drop the remaining restrictions on women in combat. In Iraq and Afghanistan, de facto, they're already gone. And finally, women's full equality under arms as citizens means that women must be included in any future draft.

It is not my intention here to write a detailed assessment of the performance of American women in the present wars.[1] However, it matters to point out that if there is to be any meaningful restoration of the linkage between citizenship and the common defense, women may no longer be excluded or barred from full participation. A lot of people won't like it, for a lot of reasons. But with women, as with gays, the fundamental issue is not who likes it. The fundamental issue is, what is required of us as citizens, if this nation is to survive and contribute to the survival of this species and this planet.

IT IS TRUE that women have participated, officially and unofficially, openly and surreptitiously, in all of America's wars. Sometimes it's hard to separate truth from legend, and even well-documented stories can challenge credulity. But the fact remains: Women were there.[2]

During the Revolutionary War, American women served openly, including battlefield time. Mary Hays McCauly, a veteran of

Valley Forge whom George Washington warranted a sergeant, was not the only "Molly Pitcher" to pour cooling water on hot artillery barrels. Others, such as Deborah Samson, took men's dress to serve; some, like Margaret Corbin, accompanied their husbands, wherever. Corbin was wounded in action at the Battle of Fort Washington. Indeed, it's worth repeating that the whole concept of an army as "men only, period" is only a few hundred years old, part of early modern European monarchy's long struggle to wrest control of their forces from feudal lords and feudal levies and their ways.

From the start, General Washington copied the British practice of including women as nurses, cooks, laundresses, and providers of other menial services. The first eight British regiments sent to subdue the colonies numbered 677 men and 67 women each. Washington allowed rations for one woman per 15 men. Often, these women were mothers, wives, sisters, or sweethearts of the soldiers. Few were prostitutes. Many sickened and died. As members, albeit unofficial, of a rebellious army, they could have been executed had the patriots lost.

The pattern continued through the Civil War, with women even serving in line regiments. Sometimes their gender was hidden, at least for a while, by sympathetic male comrades. Inevitably, they would be found out and summarily discharged, only to try their luck with another outfit. Tens of thousands probably served as fighters, nurses, menials, and spies on both sides.

And lost to history forever: Those thousands upon thousands of incidents, from the first colonies through the closing of the western frontier, when women fought with local militias, as irregulars, as pioneers, and as terrorists.

The service of 1,500 women nurses during the Spanish-American War led Congress to establish a permanent Army Nurse Corps in 1901; the Navy followed in 1908. About 33,000 women served in uniform during World War I as nurses and Navy yeomen. Others, such as French-speaking American telephone operators, known as "Hello Girls," worked as hired civilians in Europe. They enjoyed no military status but were subject to military discipline. About 400,000 women served during World War II in the various service auxiliaries: WACs, WAVEs, WMs, WASPs, and so on. Over 400 died.

As part of the postwar defense reorganization, women other than nurses finally became eligible for permanent status in the military. However, according to the Women's Armed Services Integration Act of 1948, women could number no more than 2 percent of the total force, with women officers no more than 10 percent of that. Promotions were rigidly capped above company level. Women were barred by law from Navy combat vessels and aircraft engaged in combat missions, and by policy from ground combat units. By policy also, women were denied command authority over men. In 1951, as 120,000 women started moving into wartime service during Korea, Executive Order 10240 authorized the services to discharge summarily any woman who became pregnant, had a child, adopted a child, or who had a child at home more than one month per year.

And there the situation stood until the services started looking to women for Vietnam needs. Over 7,000 served in Vietnam, more than twice as many American men as went to prison for all draft-related offenses. In 1967, the 2 percent ceiling was lifted, as were promotion restrictions. In 1969, the Air Force opened ROTC to women; the Army and Navy followed in 1972.

The rest of the decade reads like an almanac of accomplishments. In 1972, Admiral Elmo Zumwalt, then chief of naval operations, opened a wide variety of noncombat MOSs (military occupational specialties) to women, including noncombat aviation and command billets ashore. The Army opened noncombat aviation in 1974, the Air Force in 1976. That same year, Congress opened the three service academies to women (the Coast Guard Academy had already integrated). Over the next few years, women gained the right to serve on noncombat Navy vessels. The Army and Marines also expanded the jobs and assignments open to women, beginning a complex pretense that continues to the present day: that if women are "attached" to forward units, not "assigned," they're not really combat soldiers.[3] The absolute prohibition against children gradually eroded. No professional force could have maintained it.

At first glance, it would seem that the Armed Services had begun the permanent integration of women into their ranks in much the same manner as had the civilian world. Would that they had done so. It might have saved a lot of people a lot of pain, and spared the military decades of self-inflicted institutional damage. And America as a culture might have been better for it.

Conscription ended in 1973. Good people were staying away in droves.[4] Not unreasonably, the military decided that women, with their generally higher test scores and educational levels, plus their generally lower potential to become disciplinary problems, would make up the shortfalls . . . until, whether by renewed voluntarism or a new draft, the men returned. The separate women's auxiliary services were gone. Numerical caps and limits on promotions, the same. Jobs were opening up. But it was never meant to be a permanent condition. And virtually no one in the all-male senior leadership entertained any notion, drunk or sober, that women would ever be admitted to the sine qua non of military equality: combat. Their accomplishments would be noted and appreciated. But equality was out of the question.

The military's leadership did not reach this conclusion because they were bad men. Far from it. These were the heroes of three wars past. They were, as a group, intelligent and humane. But bound by their times and their own experiences, they simply could not conceive of it. Perhaps General Robert Barrow, commandant of the Marine Corps, put it best when he said, more than once, that there was something abhorrent about old men sending young women to war. Had he been asked whether it was less abhorrent to send young men to war, he would doubtless have answered, no. It was just that sending women was, for lack of a better term, different.

But the military's leadership was playing a duplicitous game. They knew full well that even though they might not send women to war, war would come to them. In Vietnam-type situations, as in Iraq and Afghanistan today, the front could be anywhere and everywhere. The military also knew, and admitted, that in any war against the Soviet Union, women would be forced into combatant roles as all those Warsaw Pact divisions slashed into supply lines and rear areas. A North Korean invasion of South Korea would have the same nasty effect. Nonetheless, all the services, and especially the Army, maintained the charade that these increasingly essential women would not be assigned to combat units, or would be removed prior to hostilities. They could therefore reassure servicewomen that they would never be in combat, and therefore need not be trained for combat.

Which meant that their male comrades could not trust them when it mattered most—in a fight. They could not trust them to be there in their normal roles. Nor could they trust them as combatants.

So why did the military maintain the pretense? It would take a team of psychologists and psychiatrists to disaggregate the rationales, defense mechanisms, and self-delusions, and I've never been much for amateur long-distance psychiatry or psychohistory. Or for psychobabble. Suffice it to say that a combination of forces was at work here, from sincere desire to spare women the horrors of war to suspicion that any European or Korean war would go nuclear so fast, it wouldn't matter. Add also a culturally determined mind-set concerning women's allegedly inherent physical weakness and other limitations, plus an inability to understand that some women might respond to the same ideals and ambitions they themselves had. And last but certainly not least: a growing contempt for a feminist movement that had nothing but contempt for them, and didn't mind saying so. James Webb, one of the Marines' most decorated Vietnam veterans, recounts that he once tried to explain to a woman lawyer why General Barrow might hold his position. The woman conceded that he knew a little bit about war. But, she sneered, "What does he know about women?"[5]

Probably, one might suspect, a lot.

To repeat: The good men who set and enforced this policy knowingly consigned women to second-class status, with all that entailed in an overwhelmingly male, strictly hierarchical institution whose raison d'être is violence. It is doubtful that they understood the full implications of what they did. Or perhaps it wasn't that they didn't know so much as they didn't want to know. They would doubtless have been horrified to learn how many women came to accept being vilified and attacked as part of the price of wearing their country's uniform. They would doubtless have been horrified to receive a letter from a parent stating, "I sent you a boy. You sent me back a rapist." They would doubtless have been horrified to learn that, from boot camps and service academies through the operating forces, what can only be described as "fragging by rape" became common. "You don't belong here. This is how we'll drive you out." In thousands of cases, it worked.

They were good men. But they were blind, willfully blind, to what they did and allowed. Or maybe it just wasn't that important to them.

Unfortunately, the not-so-good men who populated the military in the 1970s, and a sadly sizable number since, too often took this inferiority as a license for sexual harassment and worse. Too often, to this very day, the hierarchy did nothing about it or shrugged it off with the standard array of excuses. Boys will be boys. She was probably looking for it. She changed her mind later. It wouldn't have happened if she hadn't been here—where she doesn't belong, anyway.

In sum, the entry of women into the military coincided with a major post-Vietnam degradation of the good order and discipline of the force as a whole, coupled with a profound institutional aversion to facing the realities that women's second-class status virtually mandated. Certainly, every outfit has its percentage of jerks, evil-doers, and their active and passive accomplices. The issue is not their presence. The issue is: Who sets the tone? In a properly disciplined unit, the bad actors don't dare, or are quickly dealt with and/or removed. In an undisciplined unit, they can take over. Since the 1970s, it has been true that units and organizations with major sexual harassment (the predator's "foreplay") and assault problems, usually have other leadership failures as well.

Throughout the seventies and eighties, the military failed either to prepare women for the reality that they would be in combat, or to protect them from predators among their comrades. A male soldier who attacked another male soldier and put him in the hospital would be punished as a matter of course. A woman soldier who ended up in the hospital, raped and battered, would too often be told, Get over it. And rather often, Get over it and get out.

Then the feminists got interested. Big-time. Because of their involvement, the better things got for women in the military, the worse they got. In the end, it took the Iraq war—and the new generations fighting it—to begin to sort the mess out.

This is not the place for an extended disquisition on feminism: where it came from, where it went. In its nineteenth-century American aspect, feminism was a quest for full civic equality and responsibility. While the bearing of arms was rarely mentioned—items such as education, property ownership, the franchise, and divorce were far more pressing—the movement was neither inevitably pacifist nor inevitably antimale. Many feminists who were also abolitionists had no problem supporting the Civil War. By the late nineteenth century, feminism was flirting with the growing international peace movement and had acquired a definite antimilitarist tinge, although being antimilitarist is far from the same as being antimilitary or antimale. And even during its most potent era, the 1930s, promiscuous male-bashing didn't rate high on the agenda.

By the 1960s, feminism clearly stood within the farther-left precincts of the liberal camp. But it was still a relatively rational, civic-minded affair. Betty Friedan's "Problem That Has No Name," sometimes uncharitably also known as the lack of female fulfillment, would not become a political issue until after Vietnam had established the manner in which it would be expressed.

As already discussed, so much of the so-called resistance to Vietnam, and of the Movement as a whole, keyed on the quest for an unearned moral stature via an inchoate mind-set based on psychologized ethics—how I feel is what matters—and the expression of rage over victimizations and affronts past, present, and future: real, presumed, and purely fictive. Women had issues with America. America had issues with women. These formed the basis of what philosopher Christina Hoff Sommers aptly called liberal feminism. We're all in this together, but we've got some problems to straighten out. However, as liberal feminism segued into gender feminism—men are the enemy—and rational discourse gave way to consciousness-raising, emoting, and histrionics, the real issues got lost amid the culture wars rage.

Not entirely, of course. As women in their millions entered business and the professions, they came as much to change things as to participate as equals. Many of these changes were both benign and long overdue. But that quintessentially male institution, the military, could not, in their view, be changed. It was evil. Women, the naturally gentler and more benign gender (that's gonna be news to Medea), shouldn't even want to participate in the war machine. Although, suggested feminist Sara Riddick, drafting women might help "pacify the forces" they entered, few feminists ever got beyond their reflexive antimilitary sentiments.[6] Those who did, more often than not, confessed themselves "conflicted." Today, endless library shelves groan under the weight of their products. Groan, because no one reads them much anymore.

Still, by the eighties, it was clear to the well-organized and well-funded professional feminists that the military was the last bastion of machismo, and it needed to be brought down for the sake of the conquest. The feminist weapons of choice were scandal, politics, lawsuits, advocacy scholarship and pseudoscholarship, media, and hate. Beginning in the 1980s, or perhaps the latter seventies, feminists gleefully exploited every sexual and discrimination scandal the military could provide, and the military provided plenty. Posturing and hype, media exploitation and congressional hearings, academic conferences and official commissions, not to mention DACOWITS, the Defense Advisory Committee on Women in the Service. The feminists and their supporters manufactured endless demands for atonement—practical atonement that opened more and more jobs, including duty aboard combat aircraft and ships, to women. "Take the Toys from the Boys" may have been a cutesy bumper sticker slogan. "Give Them to the Girls" never quite caught on. Girls weren't supposed to want them. Not PC girls, anyway. But it was happening.

In short, by the 1980s, and certainly after the 1991 Tailhook filth, the military found itself under sustained feminist attack. It responded to the political pressures that attack engendered by meeting demands for ever-greater opportunity and equality. But it did so in a manner guaranteed to alienate the men who needed women's skills and devotion, and would soon enough need their courage in battle.

The military is a bureaucracy and, like all bureaucracies, abides by certain rules. The first and greatest is: Protect thyself. The Pentagon protects itself by keeping the politicians happy, especially the Congress that votes the bucks. Congress has to protect itself by getting reelected, and usually appreciates favors and concessions that help it do so. The Pentagon obliges. In many ways, letting women fly planes was a small price to pay for getting those planes and keeping the relevant politicos appeased. Had bureaucratic self-protection ended there, no biggie. But the bureaucracy chose to protect itself in another, far more insidious way.

During the Reagan administration's later years, the country was alternately horrified and amused to learn that the Pentagon was buying $600 hammers, $2,500 toilet seats, and $5,000 coffeepots. In truth, much of this was manifestly unfair. Some of these prices were the result of an accounting gimmick called "equal allocation of overhead" and not the actual prices. As for that $5,000 (or whatever it was) coffeepot, the thing was really an airborne hot beverage maker: a device that could brew coffee and heat water for tea, soup, hot chocolate. All in all, a very versatile machine that, at least according to legend, had been MilSpec'd—that is, designed to military specifications—to withstand forces that might crash the plane and kill the customers. But no matter. Congress huffed and posed, oversaw its oversights and enacted its enactments, both statutory and advisory. These the military translated into so many detailed orders, regulations, policies, and procedures that there would never again be a $5,000 coffeepot. As the joke went, the next crisis would involve a $10,000 teakettle.

Micromanagement. Idiotic, insane micromanagement designed not so much to solve problems as to be able to explain, when things went bad, that it was all the fault of individuals who weren't following the rules.

What the bureaucracy did about coffeepots, it did even more energetically about women. It began with the clear and cynical relaxation of standards. It went on with the institution of anonymous 800-number harassment-and-assault hotlines without providing clear guidelines on what constituted what. It proceeded to the imposition of restrictions on male-female interactions as detailed as they were looney tunes. At one Army base, it was proclaimed that male-female eye contact lasting more than five seconds constituted harassment. A Marine expeditionary unit afloat in the Pacific decreed that a man and a woman were absolutely forbidden to occupy any closed compartment together, save in the performance of their duties.

And then, in the aftermath of Tailhook, there were the witch hunts, the mass polygraphs, the wrecking of innocent careers. It was all like coffeepots and teakettles. While the fundamental problems remained and intensified, defensive hyperregulation and self-protective micromanagement provided cosmetic solutions while embittering those who had to live through this moronic reign of terror.

Trapped in the middle were the military women who had no support save a feminist movement that disdained them, and who too often had no choice save to benefit from policies and procedures that hurt the institution they loved. Military women watched the feminist assault generate situations that harmed and alienated the men who should have been their brothers.

There is no nice way to say this. Feminism may have assaulted the military for decades, but it was the military that chose its own response, in accordance with its own requirements and prejudices. The National Organization for Women (NOW) had no command authority.

Then came 9/11, and Afghanistan, and Iraq. And yet another very strange thing happened. Two strange things, actually. But then again, maybe they weren't so strange.

The first was that, at the very moment when military women were proving their value under fire, feminism shut up about them. Part of this silence may be explained, of course, by opposition to the Iraq war and to Mr. Bush personally. Part may be explained by at least a soupçon of embarrassment over some early demands (always, demands) for a Congressional Medal of Honor for Jessica Lynch, and over the spectacle of women such as Lynndie England behaving badly. But at bottom, it was as though the movement, having used servicewomen for its purposes, now cast them off as no longer worthy of regard. Victims could be countenanced. Heroes, never. You will search the Web sites and publications of what's left of the feminist movement in vain for any save the most perfunctory mention of the accomplishments of the last three years.

Meanwhile, the religious and cultural rights have launched an assault of their own . . . almost. They dare not vilify those whom they should be celebrating as heroes. Instead, they, too, ignore the accomplishments, preferring to recycle outdated studies and hypothetical arguments about what "might" happen were women sent into combat, occasional anonymous accusations and sneers, and to press the politicians for action to correct this egregious situation. But "might" does not make right, and the pols know full well what military necessity requires. President Bush, who in February 2005 announced himself opposed to women in ground combat, could withdraw them by a stroke of the pen. That he hasn't speaks eloquently to the situation.

But most curious of all, those opposed to women's equality under arms continue to denounce it all as part of the old PC "feminist agenda" to destroy the military. Like hokey wrestlers prancing around in the ring, they don't (to borrow a feminist phrase) seem to get it. The opponent has withdrawn; the audience is losing interest.[7] When Mrs. Donnelly attempted to make such points on one invitation-only military list-serve, she was vigorously refuted by military men of several generations. Included were some who checked in from Iraq and a couple who had daughters and granddaughters over there. She also discovered what I've come to think of as the Grandfather Effect.

"I don't believe in women in combat. But nobody's going to tell *my* granddaughter that she can't do something because she's a girl."

so what has happened?

Simply this.

In Iraq and Afghanistan, new generations of men and women, accustomed to equality since birth, are making up the rules as they go along, and doing it well. Familiarity may breed contempt, but it can also breed respect. As my wife, Erin, discovered covering two wars, what you lose in privacy, you gain in modesty. And when, coming out of Iraq, she realized that she'd been safer as an unarmed woman in a transient barracks filled with armed men than in a luxury hotel in Kuwait, the real meaning of civilization began to sink in.

The day-to-day success of American men and women living and

working and fighting together doesn't make the news. You never hear about the rapes that don't happen, the situations that are handled by command and peer pressure, well applied. The military, for all its rules, is essentially a shame society. Reputation matters. It grows ever more unacceptable to disparage or attack the sisters, unacceptable not because of political correctness but because of cohesion. And as the brothers learn to shun and control those who do, perhaps the command structure will move toward a more aggressive enforcement of real laws against real crimes, not mere sensitivity training or teakettle regulations. It's often said that if the people lead, eventually the leaders will follow. Perhaps, from time to time, that's also true for the troops and the generals.

None of this is to say that real problems don't remain, from physical conditioning to pregnancy and motherhood, to the task of effectively integrating the combat arms of the Army and Marine Corps. But there are, I've grown convinced, no showstoppers.

7

What the Founders Understood

AMERICA'S FOUNDERS WERE THE MOST optimistic bunch of paranoids ever to win a revolutionary war, survive the aftermath, and then contrive, as they phrased it back then, "an election of government." They were, we would call them today, conflicted. It wasn't just that they were conflicted with one another. They did, even and especially when the cause to which they'd mutually pledged their lives, their fortunes, and their sacred honor seemed most endangered. Nor was it that, as individuals, so many were conflicted within themselves. They were, although only Thomas Jefferson seems to have raised inner ambiguity to the level of an art form. It was how they handled the conflicts.

They were not paralyzed by them. Nor did they dodge their conflicts, subsuming them in some larger self-evident abstract truth, abandoning or denying messy reality. Instead, they used their conflicts to create.

It's hard to know what they really thought. The paper trail they left—the most magnificent and enduring in political history—can be mined to prove, or at least evoke, just about anything. No one ever accused them of consistency. Much of what they wrote was tactical in nature, weapons for immediate use. Much of what they wrote was abstract and visionary. The two didn't always agree. And of course, they were politicians, often writing for the sake of posterity's plaudits as well as to achieve some more immediate end. And as we all know, when dealing with politicians, their stated opinions on the subject of military service are about as reflective of their true beliefs as their pronouncements on religion. Sometimes, perhaps, they are. It's easy to mouth the conventional platitudes when you genuinely believe them, or when you haven't thought much about them. It's harder when your own experience tells you that what you're saying isn't true, but ought to be.

Religion and military service—two matters where the Founders clung to the conventional pieties, and often lived them, when all their experience told them otherwise.

The Founding Fathers thought a great deal about everything. That's why, having mastered the nuances of a matter, they rarely compromised—at least not in the "Let's just split the difference" sense. The one time they tried it, on an issue pertaining to who was human and who was property, the result was a tragedy whose legacy afflicts us still. The only reason they did compromise then was that they knew there could be no final compromise on slavery. But had they fought that battle in 1776, or in 1787, there would have been no Union to settle it later.

But if the Founders didn't compromise, and if they weren't fanatical True Believers, Enlightenment *jihadi* acting on creed, how did they do it? Why did they succeed? Why did they not end up as public spectacle, enduring the British punishment for high treason, a multipart affair, the last and least distasteful portion of which was death by hanging? How did these conflicted noncompromisers accomplish anything at all?

An obsession of Enlightenment thought provides the answer. Back then, they loved the idea that countervailing forces yielded balance, the concept of passions canceling each other out. More than the Declaration of Independence got published in 1776. Adam Smith's *The Wealth of Nations* popularized the notion of the "invisible hand" of the marketplace, the force by which self-interested men, without so intending, contributed to the common good. It's easy to forget how radical a departure his theory was from the regnant mercantilism, which held that economics was a zero-sum game; that the relevant unit was the state, not the individual; and that wealth was measured in specie, not the productive genius and potential of human beings.

Smith wasn't the only one playing with balance. Montesquieu may have developed such concepts in his *Spirit of the Laws*, as allegedly influential as they were unreadable (English is better; Montesquieu, like so many of the French *philosophes*, loses something in the original), but the term "checks and balances" originally referred to the workings of a clock. Time, useful standardized intervals of time produced by countervailing weights and gears, also fascinated the Enlightenment. When the Founders built "checks and balances" into the Constitution, that political "machine which would go of itself," they weren't separating powers. They were placing them in measured opposition to one another, striving for harmony, or at least a tolerable governance, via countervailing pressures.

This was new. Although the concept of stability and strength through the artful opposition of pressures had been known for millennia—it was, after all, the design principle of the arch—older notions still competed in their minds. There was, most notably, the "Great Chain of Being," the belief that the universe was a divinely ordained, immutable hierarchy, and that stability was preserved only through human acceptance of rank and each individual's place in it. America was far from an egalitarian society. Few, especially among the propertied Founders, had any desire to make it so, and one of the great complaints of the years between the Revolution and the

Constitutional Convention was that the wrong kinds of men were rising in power, wealth, and influence. Older theories of politics had also emphasized balance, but between hierarchically ordered social groups: monarchy, aristocracy, people. The machinery of the state reflected this balance, but it was not the balance itself.

The Founders did not so much reject these ideas as adapt them. They put their faith in the balancing of pressured opposites within a machinery that could produce results beneficial to all.

And that is how their thinking on military affairs must be understood. Discussion of the constitutional machinery and its twenty-first-century relevance will come in a bit. For the moment, it's necessary to visualize how the Founders thought about and experienced the world. The complexity of this subject, not to mention the literature upon it, is so great that an exercise in visualization, an admittedly pedantic exercise, might be useful.

Imagine, if you would, a bridge over a chasm. Visualize this bridge as the journey from colonial status to the federal republic. It's a narrow bridge. One-way only. It's easy to fall off. But the real question in the minds of the travelers is: Will the bridge stay up? For this is a bridge built upon three arches, and everything depends on the keystones, the pieces at the top that join the two halves of each arch and, by balancing their pressures, keep the bridge from toppling. If the keystones fail, the bridge collapses.

The bridge stood. Barely. Afterward, the Founders, looking back in amazement, decided that, all things considered, it was a pretty good bridge. They would not tear it down because it hadn't worked as well as hoped. Nor would they tamper with its design to achieve a greater stability. They would simply patch it up, pass it on, and hope that succeeding generations would find their own ways to use it as they crossed on journeys of their own.

Like much else about the Founders and their work, it could be inspiring and enduring because it wasn't perfect.

The first arch consisted of the Founders' understanding of human nature. One half of the arch was (by historical standards) wild optimism. Humanity, the Enlightenment believed, was infinitely perfectible. Progress, the idea that human events are going somewhere and that somewhere is good, was already a standard item of advanced thought.

On the other side was the more conventional view: Humanity was evil. People were, if not irreparably tainted by Original Sin, certainly far gone in cruelty, lust, greed, furor, vice, and folly—or they were about to be. From the Bible to *The Prince*, this was what it was all about. Virtue and goodness rarely sustain; viciousness and evil are the default positions of humanity.

In *On Revolution*, political philosopher Hannah Arendt poses a deceptively simple question. Why did the American Revolution succeed while the two other great modern revolutions—the French and the Russian—yielded tyranny, oppression, misery, and waste?[1] Part of the answer is obvious. Compared to ancien régime France and czarist Russia, the United States had relatively little work to do. There was an empire to defeat, of course. But there was no monarch to imprison, no royal family to execute. No local aristocracy. No established church. No violent sectarian divisions. No plutocracy. No great mass poverty. And there was a surprising level of agreement on how society should be ordered. Social revolution was neither desired nor sought. However, Arendt continues, the real secret was that, unlike the French and the Russians, they didn't try to change human nature. No "Republic of Virtue," no "New Socialist Man," no calling each other "Citizen" or "Comrade" while shipping one another off to the guillotine or the Gulag. The Founders took people as they found them. They were, as the German word has it, good *Menschenkenner*, judges of human beings.

Yes and no. Good *Menschenkenner* don't generally waffle between fantasies of human perfectibility and the Slough of Despond regarding human iniquity. The Founders certainly did not. Instead, they crafted a keystone of citizenship. After the Greeks and the Romans, they held that full humanity was best attained via citizenship in a free polity. Outside a polity—a polis with or without walls—no one could be completely human. Aristotle's famous dictum that man is a *zoon politikon* is too often mistranslated as "social animal."

The Founders' concept of citizenship did not, of course, exclude other relationships: family, school, social community, church, trade, business, whatever. Rather, these relationships were both valuable in themselves and empowered the person to enter the public realm and thereby to fully inhabit his own life. To the Founders as to the Greeks, citizenship meant active participation in the public world. It meant the purposeful public activity of those who were educated, economically self-sustaining . . . *and capable of providing for the common defense.* To be a proper citizen was, by definition, to be willing and able to fight, or at least to have done so in one's youth. Citizenship made you more perfect; good citizens made for a more perfect union.

In the secular sense, citizenship was where human perfectibility and human depravity met, holding together the arch of civilization.

If the first arch concerned the proper secular status of human beings—and how tragically long it has taken to extend this great truth beyond the minority that enunciated it—the second arch defined political life. Again, there were two opposing forces. One, from the Greeks through John Locke, was profoundly optimistic and humane. Politics was what people did together when they left their private realms to enter the public space and conduct the public business. It was Jefferson's joy of persuading and being persuaded; it was the public aspect of the "pursuit of happiness." The Founders did not go as far as the ancients in believing that real freedom could be found only in the public realm among one's equals. To them, home and work were the realms of inferior women, children, and slaves; to concern oneself exclusively with private affairs was to be, as they put it, *idiotes*. An idiot. But the public pleasures of the Founders were clear, especially the passion for distinction that motivated Washington and Adams, and the knowledge that the stage upon which they were acting was now the world.

Creation. Participation. Consent of the governed. They believed in these things because they were also, and of right ought to be, the active governors.

Balanced against this was a far more dismal philosophy that, as Bernard Bailyn points out in his classic *The Ideological Origins of the American Revolution*, had been largely abandoned in Britain by the latter part of the eighteenth century, but which still admonished and motivated the colonies. Here the issue was not cooperation but strife. This theory of politics, writes Bailyn, "rests on the belief that what lay behind every political scene, the ultimate explanation of every political controversy, was the disposition of power . . . the dominion of some men over others, the human control of human life: ultimately force, compulsion."[2] This philosophy, variously known as the Radical Whig, Radical Republican, or Florentine, came from the ancients through Machiavelli and a variety of seventeenth-century English and Scottish writers. OK, add here Hobbes and his overworked dictum that life without government is poor, nasty, brutish, and short, as though life with government is rich, pleasant, gracious, and long. If politics was about domination, then government's function was to keep the three major social groups—monarchy, aristocracy (or court), and people (read here, minor aristocrats and gentry)—from oppressing one another, within a divinely ordered hierarchy. Note here another aspect of this view. As Jefferson put it in the Declaration of Independence, any government can achieve this balance. Conversely, any government can become destructive of it.

But how to maintain balance in an America drifting away from such concepts of order? To the Founders, men given to politics-as-participation but well aware of politics-as-oppression—many practiced that, too—the keystone was once again citizenry. But a certain kind of citizenry. One imbued with civic virtue. Not patriotism, although that mattered. Not sacrifice, although that might come about. Rather, they sought the virtues necessary to participate in and defend the polity effectively.

Few dilemmas plagued the Founders more deeply than how to nurture and sustain civic virtue. All history, as well as their own experience, showed that virtue was a transient thing. Ardor and enthusiasm could easily turn to apathy, cynicism, and worse. But without a virtuous citizenry, politics-as-participation wouldn't work and politics-as-oppression became inevitable. But how do you gauge the virtue of the citizenry? The Radical Whigs developed a veritable checklist of danger signs. The two most prominent: excessive materialism, what they called "luxury," and *unwillingness to bear arms in the common defense.*

The first two keystones, then, were citizenship as the proper human status, and the civic virtue to make it work. The third arch supporting the journey was the Founders' understanding of what violence was, and the proper response to it.

To the Founders, as to much of the world today, many kinds of violence threatened the polity. Some came from within—crime, domestic disorder, insurrection, riot—some from without—foreign war, either invasion or unwise and unnecessary entanglements and adventures. The keystone was the citizen militia. This organization could, at least in theory, act across the entire spectrum of violence, from local policing to foreign war. Just as important, it could refuse to act. If the people were not in favor of some adventure or other, their nonattendance or their active opposition would show it. The militia was not meant to be a docile reserve of force. It was meant to be an active part of the community, and a school of civic virtue for its members. And this virtue would be inculcated, not merely through the kind of training that made a militia "well regulated" (an eighteenth-century term for "proficient in marksmanship") but as a *de facto deliberative body.* Militia members were expected to talk to one another about military and other affairs. Their blind indifference to how they might be used, was not. As two modern legal scholars, Akhil Amar and Alan Hirsch, have noted: "The militia, no less than the jury, was a public space in which people from various walks of life would come together to work on a common project critical to self-government. The militia's military function should not obscure its political character."[3]

Or, as James Harrington, a seventeenth-century political philosopher, concluded: "Men accustomed unto their arms and their liberties will never endure the yoke." In pairing liberties and arms, he was hinting at more than the ability to stand against tyranny. "Liberties" here included more than being left alone. It meant one's entire fitting-out for citizenship. It also entailed participation in decision-making, a participation not limited to voting. This certainly seems strange to people accustomed to the belief that the military's sole political function is to obey. But such was not always expected, or desired, of the militia. They were meant to be a safety valve in more ways than one.[4]

Here, then, was the bridge the Founders had to cross to get from colony to federal republic: the bridge of a virtuous citizenry, able to participate in and defend the polity. But it was not enough for the individual to be ready. He had to be organized into a military entity capable of fighting. Here history and experience collided with theory. The Founders found a way, not so much to reconcile them as to live with the tension.

IN THE BEGINNING, every colony save Quaker Pennsylvania established its own militia, which often included everybody able to fight, regardless of status. As a colony's existence became more settled, the militia evolved into a more structured affair, usually composed of all adult white male citizens who could meet at least minimal property qualifications. The militia was part of the local society. Often, musters would be preceded by church services, where the men would hear "artillery sermons" exhorting them to their duty, which included drinking, drill, more drinking, more drill, more drinking, less drill. From time to time, the militia actually had to do something. It might be called out to suppress local disorder, although more than one colonial official was surprised, or maybe not so surprised, to learn that troops weren't available because the militia were among the rioters. Keeping slaves in line was also an occasional duty.

Over time, the rigors, such as they were, of militia training and service attenuated, and a new practice came into being. While the "universal" or "unorganized" militia might legally consist of all eligible males, the "select" or "organized" militia was made up of those who showed up with their muskets and their mugs. Special volunteer militias might also be raised for difficult, distant, or extended campaigning. These were often recruited from the lower orders. As military historian John Shy remarks: "There were several classes of men, whose total number was growing after 1700, who fell outside the militia structure. These classes were: friendly and domesticated Indians, free Negroes and mulattoes, white servants and apprentices, and free white men on the move. These were precisely the men who, if given the chance, were most willing to go to war."[5] When enlistment bounties and promises of future reward failed to induce, some colonies resorted to impressment. Sending the local miscreants off to war proved an early form of social engineering. "Virginia," writes historian Harry M. Ward, "used the opportunity [of one 1740 expedition] to get rid of undesirable persons." The county courts were directed to impress any who were not freeholders or indentured servants. So successful was this policy that it was continued, and Governor Gooch could write in 1746 that there had been for three years past "a succession of recruiting officers from Georgia, Jamaica and South Carolina who carried away all the idle fellows out of a country settled only by planters."[6]

An act of the Virginia House of Burgesses made it official. The first to fight would be those who "shall be found, loitering and neglecting to labor for reasonable wages; all who run from their habitations, leaving wives or children without suitable means for their subsistence; and all other idle, vagrant or dissolute persons, wandering abroad without betaking themselves to some lawful employment."[7]

Virginia was not the only colony to enact such laws or implement such policies. Concludes Shy: "It is difficult to believe that the colonial volunteers [and draftees] of the eighteenth century had more in common with the pitiable recruits of the contemporary European armies than with the militia levies of an earlier period; nevertheless, changes in the social composition of American forces between about 1650 and 1750 were in that direction."[8]

The colonists knew it. But at least they could take satisfaction in another fact. These "volunteer" militias that did the actual fighting weren't exactly representative. But they weren't standing armies, either.

Back then, there was virtual unanimity, in the colonies and in Britain, that standing armies were bad. It was not so much the fear of military dictatorship, what J.G.A. Pocock has aptly characterized as "the small change of the standing army debate."[9] Nor was it simple resentment of the cost, or dislike for the usual combination of imperious aristocratic officers and scum-of-the-earth soldiery. It was fear that reliance on standing armies would erode the civic virtue of the citizenry. But whatever the post-Cromwellian fretting in England, the colonists didn't have to worry. There was no standing army in the colonies. Their virtue was in fact being eroded by hirelings—but no war, no problem.

By 1756, there was war. And after 1763, there was a problem. As Europe's great midcentury war sloshed across the Atlantic and morphed into yet another French and Indian War, Britain sent troops. Britain won. By its final conquest of Canada and a few other seizures and concessions, Britain ended the French threat in North America. The colonies had contributed and cooperated in their own defense. Now it was time for the British army to go home.

But the British army did not go home. Nor did Britain disarm as it had after previous wars. George III was going to become a proper centralizing monarch. And the colonies were going, after a century of salutary neglect, to assume their proper role in the imperial economy. They were to provide raw materials to the home country only;

buy finished products from the home country only; cease the smuggling and the tax evasion; and stay out of trouble by staying put—that is, to the east of the Allegheny Mountains. It was a package of restrictions that made perfect sense along the banks of the Thames. It appeared rather different along the banks of the Charles, the Hudson, the Delaware, and the Susquehanna.

For nearly a century, some historians have argued that the Revolution was all about economics: an interpretation that usually says more about the interpreters than the past. The Revolution was indeed about economics. But it was not about greed. The revolutionaries would not live as second-class human beings, their endeavors and aspirations defined and limited by others. Taxation was one issue, although the slogan "Taxation without Representation Is Tyranny" was both hypocritical and idiotic. The colonists were far more lightly taxed than the British people, most of whom weren't represented in Parliament either. Indeed, the British doctrine of "virtual representation" held that, since every member of Parliament legislated for the empire as a whole, total representation was neither necessary nor desirable. Had the British said to the colonies, "OK, elect yourself some MPs; now may we tax you?" it's not hard to figure out what the colonial response would have been.

Taxation was galling. Regulation of trade, in accordance with proper mercantile economic theory, was another affront. The prohibition of westward movement infuriated both speculators and pioneers. But using regular troops to enforce these strictures, and to punish disobedience . . . that took it over the top.

By the early 1770s, the "long train of abuses and usurpations" of which Jefferson would write in the Declaration was in place. To the revolutionaries, British policy was a conspiracy "pursuing invariably the same Object," which was to "reduce [the colonies] under absolute Despotism." And the colonists were afraid—of themselves. Their sense was that the home islands had already succumbed and that they would be next, unless they could muster sufficient virtue to oppose it.[10]

In the years prior to the Revolution, the colonists attempted to reverse the two cardinal indicators of civic decay: luxury and the unwillingness to bear arms. Urged by the Continental Congress, communities of more radical agendas attempted to revitalize their militias. Joining became a test of political stance; if you favored separation, you signed on. Results were mixed, and it soon became apparent that dealing with local dissidents, or those of insufficient enthusiasm, would be a major militia function. Again, results were mixed. Simultaneously, the colonies attempted to return to a lifestyle of virtuous republican simplicity. British manufactures, especially luxury goods, were embargoed. Decadent activities such as theatergoing and ostentatious funerals were banned. It didn't last. And, as Bailyn concludes, the Revolution came about not because the colonists were so certain of themselves, but precisely because they were not. Only revolution, they concluded, could restore their rights . . . and save their souls.[11]

But who fought the Revolution, an eight-year war that moved from New England to Georgia? By some estimates, as much as 10 percent of the population, perhaps 300,000 people, may have participated, and 25,000 died in battle, not to mention wounds and the decimation of sickness.[12] They did so in a frustrating and perilous but ultimately effective strategic mix; George Washington disciplined his temper and desires and got it right. The Continental Army, whose job it was to stay alive, worked in tandem with local militia, regular and irregular units who fought occasionally but also tended to what we would call "internal security." Sometimes the interactions got strange. Military historian Don Higginbotham recounts a 1779 New Jersey incident. A group of Tories, having completed a three-year hitch with the Brits, decided to go home to patriot territory and resume their lives. The local militia, not particularly thrilled to have them back, wanted to hang them. Things led to things. Finally, General Anthony Wayne of the continental army talked them out of it.

"The Continental Army," writes Higginbotham, "was a

restraining influence on the excesses of the militia."[13] At least, when it wanted to be.

But who were those who served? Clearly, not everybody could be good-to-go all the time, certainly not in an agrarian society with crops to tend. Some of them were the patriots of legend; others weren't.

John Adams may have remarked, after it was over, that "The Revolution was effected before the War commenced. The revolution was in the minds and hearts of the people." But when the actual fighting began, he displayed a bit less certainty. " 'We must all be soldiers,' he wrote to a Boston minister in May of 1776. Seven weeks later, when a student in Adams's law office wanted to enlist, Adams advised him, 'We cannot all be soldiers.' "[14] Charles Royster's recounting of this tale sums it up. There were indeed men of property and status who served, throughout the war or from time to time. The coterie of young officers that George Washington was able to attract and keep, Alexander Hamilton foremost among them, included some remarkable fellows. But the consensus is that the vast majority of Washington's enlisted ranks, and very likely the vast majority of the official and irregular militias, came from the lower orders, including foreigners who came to fight for pay and opportunity.[15] America had Hessians of its own.

As for the new states, when militia voluntarism failed, which it did quickly, they just as quickly reverted to their old ways. As historian L. D. Cress describes it: "After appeals to public virtue failed to produce a continuous supply of willing citizen-soldiers, they turned to the poor and disenfranchised to meet state and continental manpower needs. The unmarried sons of farmers and artisans, transient laborers, newly freed or delinquent indentured servants, and even slaves were urged, induced, and compelled into military service. South Carolina designated 'all idle, lewd, disorderly men, who have no battalions or settled place of abode, or no visible lawful way or means of maintaining themselves and their families, all sturdy beggars, and all strolling or straggling persons . . . liable and obliged to serve in one of the continental regiments of this state.' . . . All the states encouraged the poor and landless to enlist with promises of land and monetary bounties that ranged from outright grants of money and acreage to tax exemptions and deferments."[16]

And so it went for eight long years. And it would be easy to conclude that the whole affair was hypocritical, venal, and corrupt. And in some ways it was. But to assume that the poor and landless and disenfranchised who served were lacking in civic virtue, love of their country, or hope for themselves is even more hypocritical. And snobbish.

In sum, the citizen-soldier ideal hadn't worked. But neither had it failed. It had, thanks largely to a saving remnant of the upper orders and a saving remnant of the lower orders, sufficed. It had, one way or another, provided enough people, enough of the time, to get the job done. The big postwar question was: Should the system that had worked so miserably, yet succeeded, be retained, altered, or abolished?

In 1783, with memory still fresh but already beginning to sanitize and sanctify the war, George Washington penned his "Sentiments of a Peace Establishment." He who'd never much cared to depend upon militia in a fight, and who'd had more than a few harsh things to say about them, now wrote:

"It may be laid down as a primary position, and the basis of our system, that every Citizen who enjoys the protection of a free Government, owes not only a proportion of his property, but even of his personal services to the defence of it, and consequently that the Citizens of America (with a few legal and official exceptions from 18 to 50 Years of Age) should be borne on the Militia Rolls, provided with uniform Arms, and so fast accustomed to the use of them, that the Total strength of the Country might be called forth at a Short Notice. . . . [S]uch sentiments, indeed, ought to be instilled into our Youth, with their earliest years, to be cherished as frequently and forcibly as possible. . . ."[17]

A little standing army was a good thing, but the defense of the nation should fall to the citizen-soldiers. Three years later, General

Henry Knox, Washington's former chief of artillery, proposed a militia plan that would have organized virtually the entire nation into three corps—advanced, main, and reserved, depending on age and function. Knox ended his proposal:

"Every State possesses, not only the right of personal service from its members, the right to regulate the service on principles of equality for the general defense. All being bound, none can complain. . . . If the majesty of the laws should be preserved inviolate in this respect, the operations of the proposed plan would foster a glorious public spirit, infuse the principles of energy and stability into the body politic and give a high degree of political splendor to the national character."[18]

It's often said that generals are always ready to fight the last war. Perhaps Generals Washington and Knox were recruiting for the last one. (In 1945, General Marshall's musings on postwar universal service resembled Washington's and Knox's. Some ideas never go away.) Or perhaps they believed that next time it would work. Or maybe their memories were already sanitizing and sanctifying their own ordeal. Certainly, during those confederal years, the revolutionaries were beset by a sense, indeed a paranoia, that they'd won the war only to lose the peace.

It was a military failure that finally produced the Constitutional Convention. "Historians agree," writes historian E. Wayne Carp, "that [the Confederal] Congress's final humiliation occurred in September 1786: when a former Revolutionary war officer, Daniel Shays, and 1,100 debt-ridden farmers marched on the Court of Common Pleas in Hampshire County, Massachusetts, to prevent seizure of their property for the payment of back taxes, the 800 militiamen called out to defend the Court refused to act because of sympathy with the rioters." When Congress tried to requisition $530,000 from the states to deal with the rebellion, all save Virginia refused to pay. Massachusetts forbade its citizens in the Continental Army to participate, "lest they interfere with the state's own efforts to suppress the rebellion." The new United States was, for practical purposes, militarily impotent.[19]

ACCORDING TO ALL accounts, the military clauses of the Constitution—more clauses deal with military affairs than with any other aspect of governance—were debated sharply but settled quickly. The result was a splendid example of balance through opposition: Congress against the executive, the federal government against the states. But the keystone of this arch was, once again, the citizen.

We review here the relevant provisions in order to determine what, if anything, remains.

The Preamble, too often dismissed as boilerplate of no legal significance, states that "We the People," through the Constitution and its workings, "provide for the common defense." This is, as Akhil Amar and Alan Hirsch point out, both a responsibility and a right. By their interpretation, military service is one of three rights—the others are voting and jury duty—that we can only exercise together. Not everyone serves, just as not everyone votes or sits on juries. But it remains both a right and a responsibility of the People to serve.

Few would make this argument today. Some feminist and gay advocates have emphasized the rights aspect; national service mavens talk about responsibility. But the dominant sense is that defense is a service that the government provides for us. We're consumers only.

Article I, Section 8 specifies the powers of the legislative branch, laying upon Congress the explicit responsibility to "provide for the common Defence."

Congress may spend money. This, they're doing.

Congress may use this money to "raise and support armies," again, an eighteenth-century term clearly meaning "hire volunteers and professionals." As a hedge against the expanding power of these standing armies, "no Appropriation of Money to that Use shall be for a longer Term than two Years." Not exactly abided by anymore. Congress may also "provide and maintain a Navy." The two services are separated and the language is different because fleets take longer to provide and must be maintained, and because (unless you live near the water) fleets are not particularly oppressive. The Constitution does not authorize an air force, but that's an understandable omission.

Congress alone has the power to declare war, although it has not bothered to do so since 1941. This clause was never intended to preclude the president from taking military actions, only to state that the legal power to establish this condition resided elsewhere. During the debates, some members wanted to vest this power in the Senate only. The prevailing view held that both houses were necessary to ensure popular support . . . and to forestall subsequent criticism from Congress when things turned sour. This hasn't quite worked as expected.

Congress was authorized to grant letters of marque and reprisal. These were warrants and commissions issued to private persons and organizations to seize and/or destroy specified things and people from those, not necessarily governments, who'd pissed us off. These reprisals were supposed to be proportionate to whatever offense had been committed and were understood not to be full acts of war or piracy. These aren't used much anymore. Given the extensive use of private military companies in Iraq and elsewhere, maybe they should be. We could start with Halliburton and Blackwater.

Congress was authorized to make "Rules for the Government and Regulation of the land and naval forces." This they do, usually after asking the forces what they'd like. The Supreme Court usually goes along.

Article I, Section 8 also authorizes Congress to "provide for organizing, arming and disciplining the Militia, and for governing such part of them as may be employed in the Service of the United

States." The Congress also "provide[s] for calling forth the Militia to execute the Laws of the Union, suppress Insurrections and repel Invasions."

And this, to misquote Captain Ahab as the white whale got closer, is where the blubber meets the boat. The power to "call forth the militia" is the only place in the Constitution that gives the federal government any power whatsoever to compel military service, and then only through the states, and then only to meet specific *defensive* needs. In *The Federalist No. 23*, Alexander Hamilton would argue that congressional military "powers ought to exist without limitation, *because it is impossible to foresee or to define the extent and variety of national exigencies, and the corresponding extent and variety of the means which may be necessary to satisfy them*" (italics in the original).[20] In 1918, the Supreme Court would agree.

And yet *nowhere does the Constitution grant unlimited powers to anyone for anything.* To do so would have been entirely anathema to the Founders. Was there to be made this one exception, because the exigencies of war were so great? Or was this fundamental limit on federal power placed precisely because the exigencies of war were so great? Few scholars and historians have ever really asked this question seriously, let alone answered it. Most waffle. Times have changed, needs have changed. And anyway, as the legal cliché goes, "The Constitution is not a suicide pact."

Moreover, having vested the nation's military power in the state militias, Article I concludes in Section 10: "No State shall, without Consent of Congress . . . keep Troops, or Ships of War in time of Peace. . . ."

Note: Militia are not defined as full-time "troops," nor are state armies expressly forbidden. Troops may be kept in peacetime with congressional consent, and there is no explicit constitutional barrier to state armies in time of war.

Article I made the military powers of Congress extensive yet circumscribed. Article II circumscribes them further. Section 2 makes the president commander in chief of the federal forces and of "the Militia of the several States, when called into the actual Service of the United States," although since the War of 1812, no president has attempted to command troops in the field. However, when the Constitution was duly ratified, it was with the understanding that Congress would soon craft a Bill of Rights, designed primarily to further limit federal powers. One of those ten amendments, the second, has military implications, not clearly understood today. It came about because the anti-Federalists feared two very different things. One was that Congress would use its control over the militia—the only militia powers that the Constitution gives the states are to appoint officers and conduct training—to eviscerate it. The other was that Congress would create in the militia a de facto standing army, maintained by the states but under federal control.

Virginia Congressman and early critic of the U.S. Constitution George Mason warned that the militia could be so abused, by use and even by training. He feared, in effect, the excessive militarization of the militia, warning that "such severities might be exercised on the militia as would make them [the freemen] wish the use of the militia to be utterly abolished and assent to the establishment of a standing army."[21]

The final solution? Place the locus of military power within the People, not out of misguided idealism or nostalgia for a past that never was, but because it could balance other military aspects of the republic.

The Second Amendment has been the subject of an absolutely astonishing amount of nonsensical comment, and yet properly understood, it is absolutely clear.

"A well-regulated Militia, being necessary to the security of a free State, the right of the people to keep and bear arms, shall not be infringed."

Over the centuries, and especially ever since "gun control" became a hot-button issue in the 1960s, there have been two schools of interpretation, each motivated by its own agenda. One school keys on the word "militia," the other on the word "people." The militia school holds that possession of firearms is a right granted to the states for militia purposes only, and that no one not actively a member is entitled. The Constitution, they hold, says nothing about Saturday Night Specials. The other school goes with the "What part of 'shall not be infringed' don't you understand?" The right lies with the individual, regardless of militia status. And while they accept that "arms" here means small arms—no one's advocating your right to antiaircraft missiles or tanks—their belief is nonetheless absolute regarding rifles, pistols, and shotguns.

In truth, both sides are right. And wrong. The People are more than the organized militia, but also more than a collection of individuals. And possession of weaponry pertains to more than the common defense. That's why the amendment specifies "security," a term that may apply across the entire spectrum of threat, from local crime to foreign war. Legal scholar David C. Williams concludes that "the Framers wrote the Second Amendment to protect the Body of the People, an entity reducible to neither the state nor private individuals but exhibiting qualities of both. Although raised by the state, the militia is not simply a servant of the government; instead, the Framers expected that if the state should become corrupt, the militia would rise against it. And although composed of private individuals, the Body of the People is not identical to them either: it is the people acting as a unified entity for the common good, not private persons acting on their own."[22]

The militia system envisioned by the Founders never quite worked. Or perhaps it never worked because it was never really tried. Throughout the nineteenth century, both the states and the federal government kept the militia impoverished. Many units became little more than social clubs, officered by local notables, men more notable for being local notables than for any military notability. The regulars regarded them with a mixture of amusement and disdain. When serious war came, some state militia units served.

More often, the states raised special units known generically as the "U.S. Volunteers."

And yet, even as the organized state militias continued to draw the scorn of the regulars and endure the financial neglect of their governments, they were coalescing into what became known as the National Guard. How this happened is a complex and subtle tale, far too intricate to recount here. What matters is that, in a series of federal laws enacted between 1904 and 1920, the Guard was given de jure status as America's primary citizen-soldier reserve, and has ever since claimed to be the direct descendant and sole legitimate heir of the ancient militia tradition.

It is the direct descendant. But it is not the sole legitimate heir. Nor should it be. Indeed, it can be argued that the Guard has become exactly what some of the Founders feared it might become: a form of standing army, used as such by the federal government at home and abroad. This says nothing negative about its members, or about the Guard's accomplishments. It does suggest that other options for citizen participation in the common defense may now be necessary, and are becoming practicable. Before sketching a few, it's good to review the essence of the Founders' understanding of the nexus between citizenship and the common defense—an understanding that speaks to us today in ways it hasn't for well over a century.

The Founders held:

That the People as militia is the best instrument to provide for security across the spectrum of disorder, violence, and strife.

That contributing to the security of the free United States is both an unalienable right and responsibility of citizenship. Enforced or not, the right and the responsibility remain.

That the fundamental guarantee of republican freedom is and always will be the civic virtue of the citizenry, expressed in many ways but most importantly in contributing to the security of the state.

That the security of the state includes more than the common defense in the strictly military sense.

That while the right and responsibility are unalienable, this does not mandate an unlimited claim upon the citizenry by the federal government.

That while many, perhaps the majority of citizens, will find ways to shirk or minimize the discharge of this responsibility for reasons other than those of conscience, what matters in the end is that there be enough of us to carry on. And that's what the Founders were aiming at.

Enough of us to carry on.

8

Citizen Service for the Age Now upon Us

WERE THIS A NORMAL DEFENSE and public policy monograph—assuming the word "normal" can be applied to such endeavors—it would conclude with a detailed list of recommendations. There would be agenda items, bullet points, statistics ranging from the irrelevant to the imaginary, and a final peroration on how much work remains to be done, and how much more funding needed.

But for at least three reasons, this is not a normal monograph. The first is that nobody funded it, so there's no need to flack for anybody's causes or interests. A defense analyst once told me that he read my stuff because I could be honest. I didn't have any turf to protect. I replied that there were times when I wished I did. He laughed, reminding me that in Washington, D.C., turf was all around. Thanks, but no.

The second reason is that this book was written for people, not policy wonks or public intellectuals. A month or so after my fiancée returned from Iraq, we were having lunch with a couple of think tank pogues. ("Pogue," be it noted, is a military term denoting anybody who's farther from the fighting than you are.) They weren't bad people; they weren't impolite; they certainly weren't stupid. One was a Gulf War vet. And we were in agreement on the war. But as our lunch progressed, it became clear that they were assiduously avoiding asking Erin about her trip. Part of their discomfort may have been gender. At some level, most guys wouldn't really care to ask a woman how her war had gone. But it was also clear that, to them, the war was largely a matter of who was getting published and who was getting interviewed and who was getting quoted. Reality had no claim on them. The war was simply the raw material they used to demonstrate their intellectual acumen. Thus had it been during Vietnam. So it was now. Again, thanks but no.

Finally, this is not a good season for "practical" studies. In January 2006, two came out. One was done by a respected think tank, the Center for Strategic and Budgetary Analysis; the other by the National Security Advisory group, a liberal group of very senior former officials and retired officers. Both concluded that the Army was in major trouble. Defense Secretary Donald Rumsfeld denounced their conclusions as "dated," "misdirected," and "ill-informed." They do not, he said, "reflect the current situation." The Army remains "enormously capable." Army Secretary Francis Harvey even called an impromptu press conference to announce that the Army "can surge to meet any crisis."[1]

One wonders whether these two gentlemen actually expected to be believed, or were just putting up the denials because appearance must be maintained. No matter. In Washington, D.C., you learn what's going on by way of the denials.

But this book is neither for the funders nor the wonks, nor for the administration. It's for the People in their role as the militia, the repository of the final military power of the nation. Few know it, but yes, the law's still on the books. United States Code, Title 10, Section 311:

(a) The militia of the United States consists of all able-bodied males at least 17 years of age and, except as provided in section 3132 of title 32, under 45 years of age who are, or who have made a declaration of intention to become, citizens of the United States and of female citizens of the United States who are members of the National Guard.

(b) The classes of the militia are—

(1) the organized militia, which consists of the National Guard and the Naval Militia; and

(2) the unorganized militia, which consists of the members of the militia who are not members of the National Guard or the Naval Militia.

It's a definition I find inadequate. Today, the militia includes, or should include, everyone: male, female, young, old, straight, gay, whatever. That's because the ultimate organization for providing the security of the United States is us. All of us. And if it is true that the Wars of the Ways are upon us; if we can expect decades of increasing and converging troubles, from climate change and new diseases to terrorism and war, then this ancient militia takes on new relevance. If all this is so, then the Founders got it right. Their understanding of what defense and security must entail is reborn. If all of us are threatened in one way or another, then all of us must respond. But not everybody must respond in the same way, or at the same time, or for the same reasons. The Founders' formula applies. Unalienable responsibility and right, but not unlimited federal obligation. As the People's responsibility to provide for the common defense grows, the federal government does not automatically claim more and more. In fact, rather the opposite. Today, more and more of the common defense should devolve from the federal government back to the states and to the People.

This would be a fundamental reversal. Today, despite Title 10, Section 311 of the United States Code, there is no binding nexus between the people and the common defense. The federal military is a professional affair from which the People, sincere protestations of high regard notwithstanding, have turned away. And the federal military is turning away from the people. Its decision to spend its trillions on things, operated by fewer and fewer professionals, could not be more deleterious, strategically and morally.

Of course, they don't put it that way. They dare not, any more than they dare say that they don't want more people because they don't want to do any more Iraqs. But the decision is there in the ways that matter, in budgets and in force structure and in the refusal even to envision a force large enough to do even a fraction of what is now necessary, from disaster relief and homeland security to counterterrorism and nation-building, from fighting the war in the shadows to deterring or fighting that inevitable next conventional war against somebody, somewhere.

The nexus between citizen service and the national defense has been broken in many ways. It has been broken because of the increasing isolation of the military from society, and of society from the military. It has also been broken because it is not the responsibility of We the People to participate unquestioningly in undeclared wars of policy and choice. As for the nexus between the citizenry and the security of the state, writ large: After 9/11, President Bush told us all to go shopping. We did. We still are.

Perhaps President Bush should have called upon us for more. Perhaps he felt that there was no need. The professionals and the second standing army of the National Guard could handle it all. Perhaps Karl Rove reminded him that asking for participation, real participation, might prove a hard sell in Congress and a harder sell on Main Street. Or perhaps he lacked a broad enough vision of participation. If he wasn't going to ask for a draft, what could he ask for? He could ask for more voluntary enlistments. He could ask for civilian voluntarism—join your local fire department auxiliary, that kind of thing. But not much else.

But this type of indifference to our own survival cannot continue indefinitely without consequence. As Leon Trotsky once put it, "You may not be interested in the war, but the war is interested in you."

Personally, I'm sorry that he didn't ask. I'm sorry because, after the initial flush wore off and the initial furor died down, his appeal would have failed. And the failure would have told us something very important about ourselves. Not that we're irredeemably lazy or self-centered or corrupt or apathetic. We're not, or at least we can change very quickly, given a compelling reason and a workable way. The failure would have told us that the reason was not sufficiently compelling and the way not sufficiently workable. What happened on 9/11 was heinous. But in retrospect, it has proven, as that young man said about his refusal to serve during Vietnam, NOT A GOOD ENOUGH REASON to demand the reconceiving of the common defense. We were content to let George do it for us. But George will not be with us forever, and it grows ever more dangerous to expect his successors to keep telling us, "Go shopping."

Which is, of course, their way of saying, "We know best. Now stay out of our way."

The task now is to apply the Founders' understanding to the needs of the age. In essence, this means five things.

First, the active federal forces must be increased by several hundred thousand men and women. It is not reasonable to expect the present administration to do so, nor the present Congress, nor the present Pentagon. To get this kind of change, a number of factors must coalesce. It may take another disaster at home, or another war abroad (Iran?) to bring about this coalescence. I hope not. More palatably, it could require a long period of fussing and gamesmanship between a future administration willing to spend political capital on the matter, a Congress prepared to do the same, and a military at last ready to mend its ways. Much will depend on the fate of the Army's "transformation" plans. At the moment, the service is reorganizing, away from heavy divisions and toward smaller, more deployable brigades. These have been advertised as great ways to cut the supporting structure and get more soldiers into fighting billets. Perhaps. But these are one-time changes and, as every good business person knows, once you've cut all the fat, there ain't no more. The Army will also have to recognize that, while high tech can work wonders, much of what it now has to do involves people, not gizmos.

In the end, admitting the need for those several hundred thousand more people means more than growing the force. It means a fundamental change in the way the Army conceives of itself and does business.

Second, it's time to make some basic decisions regarding the National Guard. Since before the First World War, the Guard has clung to the position that it's primarily a combat force, and that it's structure should "mirror" the active Army. Not unreasonable, if the Guard is to remain a de facto second standing army, available for overseas duty in whatever wars and dust-ups come along. But this role is increasingly incompatible with its state duties. Training and equipment are different; time is limited. And as Louisiana discovered in the aftermath of Katrina, it's hard to tend to New Orleans when you're in Iraq. One option might be to specialize. Some would be available for overseas duty without restriction. Others would go only upon declaration of war. Yet others would be homeland duty only. During a career, some Guard members might circulate through all three. Others might spend all their time in one kind of unit. This builds a certain inflexibility into the structure that neither the Guard nor the Pentagon would cherish. But it would also permit more people to participate in ways more compatible with their civilian lives and commitments.

At the moment, a special commission is doing a thorough review of the Guard's mission and structure. Its final report is expected in 2007. As with all commissions, it may have either of two purposes: to study a problem to death and then do nothing, or to make radical recommendations that validate a previously chosen course of action. It's too early to tell with this one. Still, if the past is any indicator, the Guard bureaucracy and lobby, two majorly potent institutions, will try to keep on having it all. They'll demand to remain a combat force, perhaps giving up a bit of structure, while preserving their full state duties. For its part, the Army will make a lot of noise, demand and/or attempt major reductions in the Guard's combat role, then settle for only minor change.

My personal sense is that the Guard should remain primarily a federal combat reserve, and be structured, equipped, and trained accordingly. It should also experiment vigorously with a variety of ways to bring people with critical skills into uniform under various specialist programs that skip or minimize the normal boot camp experience and traditional career progressions. But the Guard can no longer be expected to do months- and year-long overseas federal deployments while maintaining an unlimited liability for state contingencies and border duty.

Third, it's time to revitalize the non–National Guard state defense forces, uniformed militias that have no federal obligation. Few Americans even know they exist. Twenty-four states currently maintain such organizations. In some states, they're known as state defense forces; in others, as state guards, volunteer militias, or military reserves.

These are not private organizations, nor are they right-wing wackos. Many state charters explicitly affirm their commitment to equality. Their websites and their members state loud and clear, "If you're a racist or a bigot or a male chauvinist, don't bring it here." These organizations exist under United States Code 32, Section 309, which authorizes state forces, commanded by the governor and reporting to the state adjutant general. And there is a bill currently before Congress, HR 3401, the State Defense Improvement Act of 2005, intended to strengthen these militias. As expected, it's languishing in committee. Hopefully, it will be reintroduced during the next Congress, and at least debated seriously.

Today, these militias respond to two needs. One is the simple fact that Guard units can't be in more than one place at a time. Indeed, the modern state militias originated during World War I, when National Guard units went overseas and left their home states without their protection. About 100,000 armed members performed domestic security tasks. They grew to 200,000 during World War II for the same reason.[2] These organizations cannot be federalized under current law. Nor can they be ordered out of their home states, although many states have reciprocity agreements (as they do regarding their National Guard units). In the aftermath of Hurricane Katrina, the Gulf states activated their state defense forces; others sent volunteer contingents.[3] Those wishing to know more may contact the State Guard Association of the United States; their website provides links to individual state units.[4]

Fourth, there is no limit to the kinds of organizations Americans can come up with, legally, to aid existing defense and security organizations. The Coast Guard auxiliary and the Civil Air Patrol provide only two examples. Often, established organizations such as police and fire departments don't like to spend time on "half-trained," too often unavailable volunteer help. But the value of training these people goes far beyond whether or not they report to some specific site at some specific time. As for the kinds of volunteer organization that now patrols our borders, nonviolently and in co-operation with the relevant authorities: not a bad idea, if done right.

Finally, there is the matter of the individual *qua* individual. I would suggest here that a certain cognizance might be in order for all of us. We who live in the Pacific Northwest, for example, know that we ought to maintain emergency equipment and supplies in event of an earthquake. Many of us do, to care for ourselves, to help our neighbors, and in the knowledge that sometimes the best thing you can do for the emergency response system is not to need it. This is something we all should do now, as members of the militia that is the American people. Another example. Why cannot CPR and first-aid instruction be made a mandatory part of qualifying for that first driver's license, and refresher training a requirement for renewal every second or third time?

In short, the common defense and the security of a free nation may be tended to in many ways. Few of them provide a blank check made out to the federal government. The fewer, the better.

But what if, all the gods and goddesses forbid, some catastrophe or defeat pushes D.C. to press for a new draft? The proper form of conscription should not and must not presume unlimited liability. And it should be based upon the fact that, except in the utmost extremity, Americans should have the right to determine the level of their own participation.

The word "conscience" derives from the Latin *con sciere*, to "know with" or to "know together." The implication is that conscience, to be socially and politically valid, must be more than, as Michael Walzer once put it, "monologue." In the matter of conscientious objection to military service, we must be able to speak to one another. But ever since the Seeger, Welsh, and Gillette cases, conscience has been, in effect, without content. One need only demonstrate sincerity. And one need only refuse to participate in all war: a much easier stance than making judgments about which wars are worth it, whether based upon religious, philosophical, or political criteria.

This is wrong. Were there a draft, I would favor opening the right of conscientious objection to everybody, no questions asked. But there would be levels of objection, tied to levels of service.

You object to being sent overseas to fight in a war of policy, or a war undertaken without declaration. Fine. Do you object to serving in the active forces as a whole?

You object to serving in the active forces as a whole. Fine. Do you object to serving in the active forces at home?

You object to serving in the active forces at home. Do you object to serving in the Guard or reserve, in their deployable units?

You object to serving in deployable Guard and reserve units. Fine. Do you object to serving in nondeployable units?

You object to serving in nondeployable units. Fine. Do you object to serving in state defense forces?

You object to serving in state defense forces. Fine. You will pay a special surtax on your income tax for the next thirty years. If you have a problem with that, please take it up with the IRS.

The Pentagon would find such a draft abhorrent and instantly decree it unworkable. But in the end, they work for us, not the other way round. And it would certainly be preferable to yet another round of hypocrisy, evasion, and resentment. And it would certainly enhance the domestic security.

PLATO WROTE THAT only the dead have seen the end of war. The history of the United States shows that only the dead have seen the end of people trying to avoid service, for reasons ranging from the most exalted to the most venal. But history also shows that, somehow, there have always been enough of us to carry on. It is no hypocrisy to assert an unalienable universal responsibility while acknowledging how few of us, in reality, will take it up. But in the end, our survival, and perhaps that of the planet, will not be determined by how equitably a burden is shared, only by how well it is discharged. We cannot predict how we will be needed, only that we will be. And in the end, the satisfaction of serving honorably and well will always outweigh the satisfaction of having weaseled out, no matter how honorable you try to call it.

But we are left with one final question: How should an individual decide what level of participation he or she desires? Obviously, many practical factors enter into such decisions. Still, there should be something more, especially if one is considering levels of participation that include foreign war.

Today, legally and culturally, conscience has no definable content. Many scholars and pundits have offered, as a means of getting thought going, the Just War theory or heritage, a combination of religious and secular thought that holds that there are specific criteria for judging the rightness or wrongness of a war. The list would seem exhaustive. Before going to war (the *ius ad bellum*, as it's known) there must be:

Just cause.

Competent authority.

Right intent.

Exhaustion of peaceful alternatives.

Some confidence that the end will justify the misery and destruction.

The part of the theory pertaining to the conduct of war (the *ius in bello*) offers a list of its own.

Proportionality of means to goals desired.

Discrimination between combatants and noncombatants.

Adherence to all the laws and conventions of war.

All very fine. But you don't have to be an average person to see that these are but checklists to be manipulated any way you choose, to reach any conclusion you desire. Those who wish to employ them are welcome to. But I prefer something a bit less mechanical, a bit less malleable.

In the end, what I find most persuasive is the cry of that young Vietnam draft dodger. *I haven't been given a good enough reason to fight.* Or to serve.

Good enough reasons. That's what we need. Sometimes, the government provides them. But the government can demand only legal obligation. It's up to each of us to determine whether legal obligation also entails moral obligation. Sometimes we provide moral obligations for ourselves, and it's up to the government—at least, it should be up to the government—to find ways to make them real.

Either way, it comes down to enough good reasons. Without them, there is nothing save coercion and/or disaster. With them, we are able to speak to one another, to know one another, and to act. But if we cannot, as a people, generate enough good reasons to serve in the twenty-first century, then we are admitting that our common survival is no longer of great importance to us. And we should not be surprised at the consequences.

Afterword

FINISHING A BOOK is an odd experience. Not finishing the writing so much as the final edits and proofs. Sending the damn thing off to the publisher occasions a variety of emotions, from explosive decompression and negative stress to a simple, sad fatigue that makes celebration unpalatable. About all that endures is the hope that maybe it will do some good.

Print freezes text. The book exists. It has entered time. But time marches on, though nowadays the more appropriate image might be of time staggering on. Late April 2006. The Bush administration has a thousand days to go. And there's a two-feet-tall stack of articles on my desk, printouts off the Internet, material that came in too late for inclusion in the text.

All the active-duty branches exceeded their (lower than last year) recruiting quotas in March.[1]

Informal chatter indicates that junior officers, captains especially, seem to be leaving at an ominous rate. This matters. Anyone
who stays in long enough to make captain or major has planned on
a military career. Leaving after eight or ten or fifteen years means
more than changing jobs. They are, to borrow an old Bolshevik
phrase, voting with their feet.

There's a report out on why the defense budget figures used by
the Congress and those used by the executive branch never seem to
agree. There's another item on why it will be several more years before the Pentagon can take, let alone pass, a standard government
audit. When the Bush administration took office, the Pentagon estimated that it couldn't account properly for well over $2 trillion in
expenditures. The administration swore to clean up this mess. Perhaps they will. A good first step would be to figure out how much
they're spending now. But no one knows, what with all those regular budgets and supplemental appropriations and add-ons and the
rest. It's like McDonald's hamburgers. They knew once, or at least
pretended they knew, how many they'd served. Now it's just billions
and billions.[2]

A GAO Report—GAO now stands for Government Accountability Office, not General Accounting Office—indicates that
twenty-five major weapons programs are now more than 50 percent
over budget estimates; some won't be fielded for decades. The Pentagon has countered that it's really not that bad, just new accounting
procedures.[3]

The news from Iraq remains mixed. Four months after their
much-praised election, they're finally getting around to cobbling
together a government. Don't they know there's a war on? Hundreds of thousands of Iraqis know there's a war on. The ones who've
been driven from their homes by rival militias know it. There are
now displaced persons camps all over Iraq and an estimated one million Iraqis in Jordan, compared to 300,000 under Saddam.[4] How
many tens of thousands does it take before the phrase "ethnic
cleansing" starts to apply?

The Iraqi Army seems not to know that there's a war on. I was astonished to learn that Iraqi recruits do not sign contracts. They're free to come and go as they please, and often do. *USA Today* quotes an Iraqi battalion commander, Col. Alaa Kata al-Kafage: "Under the military agreement, they can leave anytime. After [soldiers] get paid and save a little bit of money, they leave." An Iraqi major general, Jaafar Mustafa, adds: "We do not want any soldier to stay against his will. Because this will affect the performance and the morale of the Iraqi Army."[5] Perhaps it would be appropriate to wonder how many insurgents and militiamen signed on to get their training, and their weapons, at government expense.

The London *Sunday Times* reports that, should an Iraqi government finally form, the United States plans a new offensive in the capital, a "second liberation of Baghdad," to celebrate.[6] Meanwhile a study by the Center for American Progress, a liberal think tank, reports that the U.S. Army needs $9 billion this year and $16 billion in 2007 to start fixing and replacing equipment lost, damaged, gone missing, or just worn out in Iraq.[7]

Then there's a separate little stack on China's growing military prowess, global influence, and consumption of oil, all funded by a United States that has sold its soul for the privilege of consuming their junk. Our 2005 trade deficit hit $726 billion; we haven't run a surplus for over thirty years. Last year, the federal government spent $352 billion on interest payments on the national debt. Over $2 trillion of that debt, about half the total, is held by foreigners.[8] So what do you do when you realize that this debt (not to mention a few score trillion for Social Security, Medicare, and other entitlements) has gotten so great that it will never be paid?

You borrow more.

The Pentagon has announced that it will no longer pay bonuses for unsatisfactory work, after the GAO discovered that it had paid $8 billion in "special award and incentive fees, often without regard to performance." *The Washington Post* headlined this item, "Pentagon Ends Bad-work Bonuses."[9]

But perhaps the most interesting event this April has been the "Revolt of the Generals." To date, eight senior retired officers have spoken out against Defense Secretary Donald Rumsfeld and the conduct of the Iraq war. When the firestorm began, the Pentagon sat back and waited for the spontaneous counteroffensive from other retired officers. When it didn't come, they launched their own spin campaign, pointing out that a few malcontents among 8,000 retired flag officers did not much of a rebellion make. Rumsfeld supporters within the administration, especially President Bush and Marine General Peter Pace, chairman of the Joint Chiefs of Staff, praised him for everything from his work habits to his decisiveness. So did a number of senior officers who'd done the high-level planning for war. The press office even put out a memo, revealing that the allegedly dictatorial and bullying Mr. Rumsfeld had met with senior brass 347 times since the start of 2005, excluding e-mails and chance encounters in the men's room.[10] Meanwhile, some conservatives hinted darkly that there might be reason here to call for investigations of possible sedition. And Fred Kaplan of slate.com pointed out that, so long as these officers drew their retirement checks—legally, these are retainers, not pensions—they could be court-martialed for a variety of offenses under the Uniform Code of Military Justice.[11] Pentagon policy is that retired officers are ordered to active duty for purposes of court-martial only under extraordinary circumstances.

Then the spin machinery got down to what they hoped they could twist into the real issue: civil-military relations. Although nobody had questioned, and everybody reaffirmed, the hallowed principle of civilian control of the military, it was made to seem that any public criticism or questioning constituted a challenge, or at least an unforgivable breach of decorum. Active officers were to shut up and follow orders or resign. Retired officers were to shut up. By April's end, it all seemed over.

But it isn't over. For what happened transcends the fate of Donald Rumsfeld, or even the conduct of the Iraq war. To understand, consider an analogy.

Civilian control over the military, civilian supremacy, is a constitutional and legal absolute. Call it a marriage, with no realistic possibility of divorce or even separation. Civil-military relations are the habits, procedures, and accommodations that make the marriage work. Civilian supremacy is constant. Civil-military relations change over time.

From the Republic's beginnings to the 1960s, this relationship proved remarkably stable. For its part, the military would accept civilian control. The military has, Douglas MacArthur and a small clique of Civil War generals notwithstanding. In return, the military has expected two things. It would enjoy operational autonomy in the conduct of war, and it would be master in its own house.

For nearly half a century, these two conditions have eroded to the point of meaninglessness. Thanks to modern communications, intelligence, and other technologies, civilian leaders since Johnson and McNamara have routinely micromanaged the conduct of military operations, and not for the better. Since Vietnam our wars have been wars of policy and of choice, not clear struggles for national survival. When wars are political, it is impossible to pretend that the military should not be involved in decision-making.

Further, the military long ago ceased being able to structure and equip itself rationally. This has less to do with the institution's inherent conservatism than with the complexities and the amounts of money involved. Long ago President Eisenhower warned us of the undue influence exerted by the "military-industrial complex." Today, that influence has thoroughly corrupted defense planning and structuring. Put simply, the Pentagon orders what the arms makers peddle and the Congress ponies up the money, regardless of real-world needs and priorities. It's nuts. But it's a profitable insanity, with profit measured in corporate bottom lines, military and congressional careers, and postretirement opportunities for all who go along and get along. This, too, is political.

This book has been about restoring the relationship between the citizenry and the common defense. America needs citizen-soldiers.

But we also need soldier-citizens, especially senior retired officers and younger vets who will speak out across the whole spectrum of civil-military relations. The Generals' Revolt of spring 2006, although aimed at the Bush administration, also set a precedent. It began a conversation between the military and the American people that should and must continue and expand, if the American people are to reconnect with a rational and effective common defense.

Will it continue? Who knows? For the moment, that's a matter best left to my next book, *Closing Ranks: America Reconnects with Its Military*. But I do find in my pile of recent articles, two items. On April 20, 2006, the *New York Times* ran an op-ed piece by a young Marine Iraq veteran, Paul Kane. "The American people," he began, "need to be prepared for what is shaping up to be a clash of colossal proportions between the West and Iran." Because of this, the administration and Congress should "reinstitute selective service" in lottery form, for men and women and without deferments. Mr. Kane contends that such an action would send a strong signal of resolve to the world, the kind we failed to send after 9/11, and concludes: "We should not fumble the opportunity now to begin selective service again. . . . It may be our last best chance to avoid war with Iran."[12]

Whether Iran would be deterred, or anybody else impressed, by a new draft may be debated. Whether Mr. Bush would propose such a move in a crucial election year, with his administration's fate hanging in the balance, does not seem likely. Still, also on April 20, 2006, the Associated Press put out a short feature headlined, "DRAFT BOARDS STAY READY—JUST IN CASE."[13]

P.S.

ONE DAY AFTER CLASS, a student came up to me with a look of frustration on her face.

"Problem?" I asked.

"I'm frustrated," she said.

"Anything in particular?"

"No. Yes."

"What?"

"Everything. Nothing."

Knowing that when people are genuinely upset, they start using words like "everything" and "nothing," I asked her to explain.

"Your lectures."

"All of them?"

"Yes. What I mean is, I can see where you're going. That's clear enough. But you say something and it raises a question. Then you say something else and I get another question. Pretty soon, I can see the conclusion. But all I've got is a mess of questions."

I smiled.

"Thank you," I said.

"For what?"

"For telling me that I've been doing my job. That's exactly the response I hope for."

If you've made it to the end of this, and have far more questions than answers . . . thank you.

Notes

A note on notation. The vast majority of the newspaper and periodical articles cited below came off the "Early Bird," the Pentagon's in-house electronic news service, or off two private list-serves. These generally stripped away the original Internet IDs and either substituted their own or added none. Since these are restricted-access, I saw no reason to put down their IDs and access dates. Also, the *Chicago Manual of Style* is a crime against humanity and a stench in the nostrils of the Lord.

INTRODUCTION

1. For that strange tale, please see Philip Gold, *Take Back the Right: How the Neocons and the Religious Right Have Betrayed the Conservative Movement* (New York: Carroll & Graf, 2004).
2. See Francis Fukuyama, "The End of History?," *National Interest* (Summer 1989): 3–18.

MISE-EN-SCÈNE

1. For a few examples, please see Philip Gold, *Against All Terrors: This People's Next Defense* (Seattle: Discovery Institute Press, 2002) and Philip Gold, "To Guard an Era: American Purpose after Iraq," *Proceedings of the U.S. Naval Institute*, September 2003, 18–22.

CHAPTER ONE: THE CRISIS THAT ISN'T . . . OR IS IT?

1. Francis J. Harvey, "No Recruitment Crisis for the Army," *Washington Post*, October 21, 2005, 22.
2. Bill Gertz and Rowan Scarborough, "Inside the Ring: Not Broken," *Washington Times*, December 22, 2006. I'd seen the actual letter, circulated by e-mail,

a couple of weeks before. The subject line read: "The ARMY is not BRO-KEN." The tone was, to say the least, agitated.

3. Michael Levenson, "Guard Pays Members for Enlisting Others," *Boston Globe*, January 5, 2006. See also Jen DiMascio, "Schoomaker Articulates Philosophy for a 'Fully Resourced Army,'" *Inside the Army*, January 16, 2006, 1.

4. Ann Scott Tyson, "Army to Halt Call-Ups of Inactive Soldiers," *Washington Post*, November 18, 2005, A-11. See also Associated Press, "Army to Expel No-Show Troops," *Washington Times*, January 10, 2006.

5. U.S. Department of Defense, phone query 10960: Members Deployed as of October 2005, CTS Deployment File.

6. DiMascio, "Schoomaker Articulates Philosophy."

7. Kim Gamel, "U.S. Air Force's Role Changing in Iraq," *Washington Post*, January 2, 2006.

8. David Lerman, "Changing Course: Navy's Plans for Fighting Terror Call for Smaller Ships," *Newport News Daily Press*, December 13, 2005.

9. Jason Sherman and Daniel G. Dupont, "Pentagon to Retire B-52s, U-2s, and F-117s in Bid to Save $16.4 Billion," InsideDefense.com, January 9, 2006.

10. U.S. Department of Defense Fact Sheet, Active Duty Military Personnel by Rank/Grade, October 31, 2005. See also Jim Hodges, "General Prepares to Do Battle with the Numbers," *Newport News Daily Press*, December 29, 2005, 1.

11. For a few examples of creative noncomprehension, see Elaine M. Grossman, "Air Force 'Mission Statement' Leaves Many Officials, Experts Baffled," *Inside the Pentagon*, December 15, 2005.

12. U.S. Department of Defense, News Release No. 1260-05, "Rumsfeld Appoints Retired Four-Star to Lead IED Effort," December 5, 2005.

13. Rato Bishnoi, "England Establishes 'Joint IED Defeat' Office, Replacing Task Force," *Inside the Army*, January 23, 2006, 10.

14. "DOD Plans $5B in Spending to Fight IEDs by End of '06," *Aerospace Daily & Defense Report*, April 6, 2006. See also Jason Sherman, "DoD Plans New Roads to Avoid Iraqi IEDs," InsideDefense.com NewsStand, February 24, 2006.

15. Nigel Aylwin-Foster, "Advice from an Ally: Get Past the Warrior Ethos," *Washington Post*, January 15, 2006, B-3.

16. Damien Cave, "Vital Military Jobs Go Unfilled, Study Says," *New York Times*, November 18, 2005.

17. UPI, "Army Gives $500m Re-enlistment Incentives," December 16, 2005.

18. Jeff St. Onge, "Family Costs Press Pentagon as More Soldiers Have Spouses, Kids," Bloomberg.com, December 29, 2005.

19. Pamela Hess, "19,000 Fewer Young Soldiers than in 2001," UPI, January 27, 2006.

20. James Hosek, Jennifer Kavanagh, and Laura Miller, *How Deployments Affect Service Members* (Santa Monica: RAND Corporation, 2005).

21. Figures from U.S. Department of Defense, Office of the Undersecretary of Defense (Comptroller), *National Defense Budget Estimates for FY 2006* (Washington, D.C.: GPO, 2005), 217.

22. Jason Sherman, "Rumsfeld to Senior Leaders: Consider 'Instructive' Perspectives on Defense Spending," InsideDefense.com, January 4, 2006. Most likely, even this superifical and silly comparison is invalid, since it involves only Defense Department spending, not total national security spending.

23. U.S. Department of Defense, *Quadrennial Defense Review* (Washington, D.C.: GPO, 2001), 17.

24. The White House, *National Security Strategy of the United States of America* (Washington, D.C.: GPO, 2002), 3.

25. Ibid., 9–10.

26. U.S. Department of Defense, Office of the Secretary of Defense, *National Defense Strategy of the United States of America* (Washington, D.C.: GPO, 2005), 16.

27. U.S. Department of Defense, Directive 3000.5, November 28, 2005, 2.

28. "England Orders Eight QDR Spin-Off Reviews," InsideDefense.com, January 10, 2006. See also "On Target," *Defense News*, February 6, 2006.

29. Rebecca Christie, "Pentagon Study Dodges Questions, Gets Credit for Answers," Dow Jones Newswires, no date.

30. Office of the Secretary of Defense, U.S. Department of Defense, *Quadrennial Defense Review Report* (Washington, D.C.: GPO, 2006), iii–vii.

31. Ibid, 25–26.

32. Ibid, 9, 23, 29–30.

33. Ibid, 38, 41.

34. Ibid, 4.

35. Ibid, 42.

36. Lawrence J. Korb, Caroline P. Wadhams, and Andrew J. Grotto, *Restoring American Military Power: A Progressive Quadrennial Defense Review* (Washington, D.C.: Center for American Progress, 2006), 3, 44.

37. The White House, *The National Security Strategy of the United States of America* (Washington, D.C.: GPO, 2006), 44, ii.

38. Fred Kaplan, "How Low Can Army Recruiters Go?," Slate.com, January 9, 2006.

39. The original article was by Mark Sappenfield, "Short of Recruits, Army Redoes Its Math," *Christian Science Monitor*, December 15, 2005. Secretary Harvey's letter appeared in the December 27 issue.

40. Lolita C. Baldor, "Army Meets December Recruiting Goal," *Washington Post*, January 10, 2006.

41. Tom Bowman, "Army Accepts Crime in Recruits," *Baltimore Sun*, February 14, 2006.

42. Greg Jaffe, "To Keep Recruits, Boot Camp Gets a Gentle Revamp," *Wall Street Journal*, February 15, 2006, 1.

CHAPTER TWO: THE PANIC THAT WASN'T . . . OR WAS IT?

1. Herbert has written often on this subject, most recently in Bob Herbert, "Sharing the Sacrifice, or Ending It," *New York Times*, December 8, 2005.

2. Oren Rawls, "Patriotic Guilt," *Los Angeles Times*, November 3, 2005.

3. Erik W. Robelen, "Draft Talk Worries Generation That Hasn't Seen One," *Washington Post*, November 3, 2004, 29, 31.

4. Franklin Stevens, *If This Be Treason: Your Sons Tell Their Own Stories of Why They Won't Fight for Their Country* (New York: Wyden, 1970), 1, 25, 85.

5. *Report of the President's Commission on an All-Volunteer Force* (New York: Collier, 1970), 11–25.

6. Martin Anderson, ed. *Registration and the Draft Proceedings of the Hoover-Rochester Conference on the All-Volunteer Force* (Stanford: Hoover Institution Press, 1982), 141.

7. See Philip Gold, *Advertising, Politics and American Culture: From Salesmanship to Therapy* (New York: Paragon, 1987), 107.

8. James Fallows, "Why the Country Needs It," *Atlantic Monthly*, April 1980, 44–47. Reprinted in Berger, *The Military Draft*, 75.

9. This growing realization was given a substantial boost by the most successful weapons system never built, Reagan's Strategic Defense Initiative (SDI) or, in the popular lexicon, the "Star Wars" antiballistic missile system. When teaching this subject to my undergraduates, I asked them to posit a fully generated system that could stop up to 30 percent of incoming Soviet warheads. Not that impressive by "One Nuke Can Ruin Your Whole Day" standards, but . . . which 30 percent? Dealing with the complexity of the countermeasures/targeting problem could have bankrupted the Soviets. Their own military-industrial complex ultimately did.

10. Charles C. Moskos, *A Call to Civic Service: National Service for Country and Community* (New York: Free Press, 1988), xi.

11. Ibid., 174.

12. For representative examples of the national service literature and debate during this period, see: Richard Danzig and Peter Szanton, *National Service: What Would It Mean?* (Lexington, Mass.: Lexington Books, 1986); Williamson M. Evers, ed., *National Service: Pro and Con* (Stanford, Calif.: Hoover Institution Press, 1990), and Eric B. Gorham, *National Service, Citizenship, and Political Education* (Albany: State University of New York Press, 1992).

13. Charles B. Rangel, "Bring Back the Draft," *New York Times*, December 31, 2002. Reprinted in *United We Serve: National Service and the Future of Citizenship*, edited by E.J. Dionne, Jr., et al. (Washington, D.C.: Brookings Institution Press, 2003), 13–17.

14. Clyde Haberman, "NYC; Draft Talk, But Source Is Antiwar," *New York Times*, January 3, 2003.

15. Caspar W. Weinberger, "Dodgy Drafters," *Wall Street Journal*, January 10, 2003. Reprinted in Dionne et al., *United We Serve*, 138–40.

16. John Cloud, "How the Draft Rumor Got Started," Time.com, October 18, 2004.

17. Edward Epstein, "Pentagon Tries to Squelch Rumors of a New Draft," *San Francisco Chronicle*, July 9, 2004.

18. "Peace Churches Warn of 'Back-door Draft,'" *Christian Century*, April 5, 2005, 15. See also "Brethren to Revive Alternative Service Plans," *Christian Century*, January 25, 2005, 15.

19. Christopher Cooper, "Rumors of Draft Are Hard to Kill Despite Denials," *Wall Street Journal*, September 27, 2004, B-1.

20. See Tony Perry, "Whites Account for Most of Military's Fatalities," *Los Angeles Times*, September 24, 2005. See also Rick Maze, "Ethnic Makeup of Military Differs from U.S. Society as a Whole," *Navy Times*, September 23, 2005.

21. Tim Kane, "Who Bears the Burden? Demographic Characteristics of U.S. Military Recruits Before and After 9/11," Heritage Foundation Center for Data Analysis Report #05-08, November 7, 2005.

22. Anita Danes, "View Misrepresents Study," *USA Today*, December 5, 2005, 14.

23. Kathy Roth-Douquet and Frank Schaeffer, *AWOL: The Unexcused Absence of America's Upper Classes from Military Service—and How It Hurts Our Country* (New York: Collins Books, 2006), 6.

24. Lawrence M. Baskir and William A. Strauss, *Chance and Circumstance: The Draft, the War, and the Vietnam Generation* (New York: Knopf, 1978), 5.

25. At www.sss.gov.

26. Phillip Carter and Paul Glastris, "The Case for the Draft," *Washington Monthly*, March 2005.

CHAPTER THREE: CONSCRIPTION CORRUPTS

1. Harry A. Marmion, *Selective Service: Conflict and Compromise* (New York: John Wiley & Sons, 1968), 24, 27.

2. See Bernard Nalty, *Strength for the Fight: A History of Black Americans in the Military* (New York: Free Press, 1986).

3. See Allan Bérubé, *Coming Out Under Fire: The History of Gay Men and Women in World War Two* (New York: Free Press, 1990).

4. In *Lawrence v. Texas*, the Supreme Court ruled that the state has no compelling reason to criminalize homosexual activity. Under the present Uniform Code of Military Justice, which is established by Congress, homosexual acts remain criminal. So do adultery and heterosexual sodomy. The Supreme Court has held numerous times that, in matters pertaining to the regulation of the military, it defers to Congress, which in turn defers to the military's interpretation of its own special needs. Whether homosexual exclusion remains a compelling military need may be, and should be, debated.

5. Lee A. Iacocca with William Novak, *Iacocca: An Autobiography* (New York: Bantam, 1984), 20

6. "Washington to the Continental Congress, 24 September 1776," in *The Draft and Its Enemies: A Documentary History*, edited by John O'Sullivan and Alan M. Meckler (Urbana: University of Chicago Press, 1974), 17.

7. "Washington to the Continental Congress, 1778," ibid., 18.

8. John G. Fitzpatrick, ed., *The Writings of George Washington*, vol. 8 (Washington, D.C.: GPO, 1933), 78.

9. This book deals primarily with the military aspects of the constitutional settlement and subsequent basic enabling legislation. The subject of military organization between the 1790s and 1812 is too complex and specialized to address here. However, there are many excellent and accessible books that demonstrate how clearly twenty-first-century issues were also eighteenth- and nineteenth-century issues. See for example, Theodore J. Crackel, *Mr. Jefferson's Army: Political and Social Reform of the Military Establishment, 1801–1809* (New York: New York University Press, 1987), and Lawrence Delbert Cress, *Citizens in Arms: The Army and the Militia in American Society to the War of 1812* (Chapel Hill: University of North Carolina Press, 1982).

10. "Webster's Anticonscription Speech," in O'Sullivan and Meckler, *The Draft and Its Enemies*, 44–50.

11. Quoted in Alan Forrest, "*La patrie en danger*: The French Revolution and the First *Levée en masse*," in Daniel Moran and Arthur Waldron, eds., *The People in Arms: Military Myth and National Mobilization since the French Revolution* (Cambridge: Cambridge University Press, 2003), 13–14.

12. Daniel Moran, "Introduction: The Legend of the Levée en masse," in *The People in Arms: Military Myth and National Mobilization since the French Revolution*, edited by Daniel Moran and Arthur Waldron (Cambridge: Cambridge University Press, 2003), 2.

13. For an excellent study of the state/federal militia/army aspects of the era, see C. Edward Skeen, *Citizen Soldiers in the War of 1812* (Lexington: University Press of Kentucky, 1999).

14. See John Whiteclay Chambers II, "American Views of Conscription and the German Nation in Arms in the Franco-Prussian War," in Moran and Waldron, *The People in Arms*, 75–99.

15. Peter Levine, "Draft Evasion in the North during the Civil War, 1863–1865," *Journal of American History* 67, no. 4 (March 1981): 816.

16. Albert Burton Moore, *Conscription and Conflict in the Confederacy* (New York: Macmillan, 1924), 28–30.

17. Ibid., 355–361. This is an old study; there may be more recent and more accurate estimates.

18. John Whiteclay Chambers II, *To Raise an Army: The Draft Comes to Modern America* (New York: Free Press, 1987), 51.

19. Ibid., 52.

20. James W. Geary, *We Need Men: The Union Draft in the Civil War* (Dekalb: Northern Illinois University Press, 1991), 66.

21. Ibid., 83–85.

22. See Roger B. Taney, "Thoughts on the Conscription Law of the United States," in *The Military Draft: Selected Readings on Conscription*, edited by Martin Anderson with Barbara Honegger (Stanford: Hoover Institution Press, 1982), 207–218.

23. Hugo G. Earnhart, "Commutation: Democratic or Undemocratic?," in *Recruiting, Drafting and Enlistng: Two Sides of the Raising of Military Forces,* edited by Peter Karsten, (New York: Garland, 1998), 233.

24. Michael Pearlman, *To Make Democracy Safe for America: Patricians and Preparedness in the Progressive Era* (Urbana: University of Illinois Press, 1984). See also Jack C. Lane, *Armed Progressive: General Leonard Wood* (San Rafael: Presidio, 1978).

25. Munroe Smith, "Democratic Aspects of Universal Military Service," in *Why Should We Have Universal Military Service?* Columbia War Papers, Series 1, No. 13 (New York: Division of Intelligence and Publicity, Columbia University, 1917), 9.

26. Quoted in Pearlman, 45.

27. Quoted in David M. Kennedy, *Over Here: The First World War in American Society* (New York: Oxford University Press, 1980), 145.

28. Pearlman, 59, 267.

29. Quoted in Gerald T. Dunne, *Grenville Clark: Public Citizen* (New York: Farrar, Straus & Giroux, 1986), 39.

30. See Chambers, *To Raise an Army,* 125–177.

31. Kennedy, *Over Here,* 144.

32. Mark Sullivan, *Our Times,* vol. 5, *Over Here 1914–1918* (New York: Scribner's, 1936), 286.

33. Michael Pearlman, "Leonard Wood, William Muldoon and the Medical Profession: Public Health and Universal Military Training," *The New England Quarterly* 52:3 (September 1979), 331–332.

34. Daniel J. Kevles, "Testing the Army's Intelligence: Psychologists in the Military in World War I," *Journal of American History* 55:3 (December 1968) p. 569. See also John Carson, "Army Alpha, Army Brass, and the Search for Army Intelligence," *Isis* 84:2 (June 1993), 278–309.

35. John T. MacCurdy, M.D., *War Neuroses* (Cambridge: At the University Press, 1918), 129–130.

36. Daniel J. Kevles, "Testing the Army's Intelligence: Psychologists in the Military in World War I," *Journal of American History* 55, no. 3 (December 1968): 569. See also John Carson, "Army Alpha, Army Brass, and the Search for Army Intelligence," *Isis* 84 no. 2 (June 1993): 278–309.

37. Quoted in Kennedy, *Over Here 1914–1918,* 150.

38. Sullivan, *Over Here 1914–1918,* 432–433.

CHAPTER FOUR: THE REAL DRAFT WILL NEVER GET IN THE BOOKS

1. Reprinted from the October 1975 *Washington Monthly* in A. D. Horne, ed., *The Wounded Generation: America after Vietnam* (Englewood Cliffs, N.J.: Prentice-Hall, 1981), 15–29.

2. Gary L. Wamsley, "Decision-making in Local Boards: A Case Study," in Roger W. Little, ed., *Selective Service and American Society* (New York: Russell Sage Foundation, 1969), 87, 97.

3. See George Q. Flynn, *The Mess in Washington: Manpower Mobilization in World War II* (Westport: Greenwood Press, 1979).

4. "Selective Draft Law Cases," in O'Sullivan, EP, *The Draft and Its Enemies,* 141, 149.

5. See J. Garry Clifford and Samuel R. Spencer, Jr., *The First Peacetime Draft* (Lawrence: University Press of Kansas, 1986).

6. Quoted in Gerald T. Dunne, *Grenville Clark: Public Citizen* (New York: Farrar, Straus & Giroux, 1986), 39.

7. Exchange quoted in Gerald T. Dunne, *Grenville Clark: Public Citizen* (New York: Farrar, Straus & Giroux, 1986), 122–123.

8. Clifford and Spencer, *First Peacetime Draft,* 1–4.

9. George Q. Flynn, *The Draft, 1940–1973* (Lawrence: University Press of Kansas, 1993), 29.

10. Ibid, 31–33.

11. Ibid, 41.

12. Ibid, 64.

13. Lewis B. Hershey, "Establishing Selective Service," A Howard Crawley Memorial Lecture (Philadelphia: University of Pennsylvania Press, 1942), 14.

14. Eli Ginzberg et al, *The Lost Divisions* (New York: Columbia University Press, 1959), 35–6.

15. See Gerald N. Grob, "The Forging of Mental Health Policy in America: World War II to New Frontier," *Journal of the History of Medicine and Allied Sciences* 42 (October 1987), 413–414.

16. John W. Appel, " 'If You Gotta Go, You Gotta Go' Is What They Replied When I Asked," *American Heritage* 50:6 (October 1999), Internet.

17. See George Q. Flynn, "American Medicine and Selective Service in World War II," *Journal of the History of Medicine and Allied Sciences* 42 (July 1987), 305–326.

18. See Paul Fussell, *Wartime: Understanding and Behavior in the Second World War* (New York: Oxford University Press, 1989), passim.

19. First Report of the Director of Selective Service, *Selective Service in Peacetime: 1940–41* (Washington, D.C.: Government Printing Office, 1942), 97, 83.

20. Second Report of the Director of Selective Service, *Selective Service in Wartime: 1941–42* (Washington, D.C.: Government Printing Office, 1943), 329.

21. The 3rd Report of the Director of Selective Service, *Selective Service as the Tide of War Turns: 1943–1944* (Washington, DC: Government Printing Office, 1945), 135, 166, 212–13.

22. The 4th Report of the Director of Selective Service, *Selective Service and Victory: 1944–1945* (Washington, D.C.: Government Printing Office, 1948), 197, 59.

23. *Selective Service in Peacetime,* 104–05.

24. *Selective Service in Wartime,* 172.

25. *Selective Service as the Tide of War Turns*, 24.

26. Quoted in George Q. Flynn, *Lewis B. Hershey: Mr. Selective Service* (Chapel Hill: University of North Carolina Press, 1985), 180.

CHAPTER FIVE: RESISTANCE IS NOT FUTILE

1. George Q. Flynn, *Lewis B. Hershey: Mr. Selective Service* (Chapel Hill: University of North Carolina Press, 1985), xiii–xiv.

2. Selective Service Figures, www.sss.gov.

3. George Walton, *The WASTED Generation* (New York: Chilton, 1965), 15, 95.

4. Little, *Selective Service*, 47.

5. See George Q. Flynn, *Lewis B. Hershey: Mr. Selective Service* (Chapel Hill: University of North Carolina Press, 1985). I was astonished, when looking at the pictures in this book, to discover that General Hershey had been young once. We always assumed that he'd been born at age geriatric, sitting in that SSS chair.

6. Jean Carper, *Bitter Greetings: The Scandal of the Military Draft* (New York: Grossman, 1967), 95–96.

7. Reprinted in Thomas Reeves and Karl Hess, *The End of the Draft* (New York: Random House, 1970), 193–200.

8. Flynn, *The Draft*, 173.

9. Lawrence M. Baskir and William A. Strauss, *Chance and Circumstance: The Draft, the War, and the Vietnam Generation* (New York: Knopf, 1978), 5.

10. Michael S. Foley, *Confronting the War Machine: Draft Resistance during the Vietnam War* (Chapel Hill: University of North Carolina Press, 2003), 49.

11. Mark Helprin, "I Dodged the Draft and I Was Wrong," *Wall Street Journal,* October 16, 1992, A-14.

12. See B. G. Burkett and Glenna Whitley, *Stolen Valor: How the Vietnam Generation Was Robbed of Its Heroes and Its History* (Dallas: Verity Press, 1998). See also Christian C. Appy, *Working-Class War: American Combat Soldiers and Vietnam* (Chapel Hill: University of North Carolina Press, 1993).

13. "Resolution of the Continental Congress, July 18, 1775," in O'Sullivan and Meckler, *The Draft and Its Enemies*, 12–12.

14. Peter Brock, *Pacifism in the United States: From the Colonial Era to the First World War* (Princeton: Princeton University Press, 1968).

15. Walter Guest Kellogg, *The Conscientious Objector* (New York: Boni and Liveright, 1919), 66–68.

16. Ibid., 70–71.

17. Ibid., 71–73.

18. Arthur Dunham, "The Narrative of a Conscientious Objector," in *These Strange Criminals: An Anthology of Prison Memoirs by Conscientious Objectors from the Great War to the Cold War*, edited by Peter Brock (Toronto: University of Toronto Press, 2005), 134.

19. J. K. Osborne, *I Refuse* (Philadelphia: Westminster Press, 1971), 45–46.

20. Three cases during the war established the current legal understanding of conscientious objection. They are:

    United States v Seeger 380 U.S. 161 (1965)

    Welsh v United States 398 U.S. 333 (1969)

    Gillette v United States 401 U.S. 437 (1971)

21. Quoted in Philip Gold, *Evasions: The American Way of Military Service* (New York: Paragon, 1985), 31–33.

CHAPTER SIX: THE WOMAN QUESTION

1. Full disclosure time. Whilst writing this book, my fiancée, Erin Solaro, was engaged in writing her own, *Women in the Line of Fire*. Many intense conversations came and went, and came and went again. This chapter is deeply indebted to her work and insights. Since *Women in the Line of Fire* is in manuscript as of this writing, there's no sense footnoting. The book provides ample documentation and bibliography.

2. For an excellent précis, see Lory Manning, *Women in the Military: Where They Stand*, 5th ed., (Washington, D.C.: WREI, 2005). Lory, a retired Navy captain, is a former graduate student of mine. Good job, Lory.

3. Since the seventies, the Defense Department and the Army have used and discarded a number of policies to determine how far forward women could go, and whether they would be withdrawn in event of war. By the latter seventies, it was apparent that combat units were now irrevocably dependent upon women as inteltypes, communicators, techs and mechanics, drivers, you name it. When Congressman Duncan Hunter, Republican chairman of the House Armed Services Committee, tried to have women in Iraq moved rearward in the spring of 2005, the Army instantly and openly opposed him. The situation is now "under study."

4. A necessary caveat here. The term "good" means, by and large, high-scoring on the aptitude tests, educational level, etc. By these indices, standards fell. But many thousands of genuinely good people entered during those years, often to leave in disgust. And even though high-quality people don't usually join failing institutions, the military remains an honorable calling, no matter what the condition of the peacetime institution. I recall attending a D.C. cocktail party in 1980, in the midst of the Iranian hostage crisis. A diplomat mentioned that the Foreign Service was no longer getting the best people, due to the perceived threats. When I suggested that maybe they were, that willingness to run such risks might matter more than test scores or fancy diplomas, he quickly changed the subject.

5. James Webb, "Women Can't Fight," *Washingtonian*, November 1979, 144–148, 273, 275, 278, 280, 282.

6. See Sarah Ruddick, "Pacifying the Forces: Drafting Women in the Interests of Peace," *Signs* 8, no. 3 (Spring 1983): 471–489.

7. Those wishing to track these arguments should start with www.bible-research.com/women/women-in-combat.html.

CHAPTER SEVEN: WHAT THE FOUNDERS UNDERSTOOD

1. Hannah Arendt, *On Revolution* (New York: Penguin, 1963), passim.
2. Bernard Bailyn, *The Ideological Origins of the American Revolution* (Cambridge: Harvard University Press, 1967), 55, 56.
3. Akhil Reed Amar and Alan Hirsch, *For the People: What the Constitution Really Says About Your Rights* (New York: Free Press, 1998), 133.
4. Quoted in J.G.A. Pocock, ed., *The Political Works of James Harrington* (Cambridge: Cambridge University Press, 1977), 443.
5. John Shy, *A People Numerous and Armed: Reflections on the Military Struggle for American Independence* (New York: Oxford University Press, 1976), 29.
6. Harry M. Ward, *"Unite or Die": Intercolony Relations 1690–1763* (Port Washington, N.Y.: Kennikat Press, 1971), 109.
7. Quoted in Shy, *People Numerous and Armed*, 30.
8. Ibid.
9. Pocock, *Harrington*, 131.
10. Bailyn, 133–143.
11. IBID
12. Estimates of population and casualties vary wildly. Perhaps the best is Howard Peckham, ed., *The Toll of Independence: Engagements and Battle Casualties of the American Revolution* (Chicago: University of Chicago Press, 1974).
13. Don Higginbotham, "The American Militia: A Traditional Institution with Revolutionary Responsibilities," in *Reconsiderations on the Revolutionary War: Selected Essays* (Westport, Conn.: Greenwood Press, 1976), 101.
14. Charles Royster, *A Revolutionary People at War: The Continental Army and American Character, 1775–1783* (Chapel Hill: University of North Carolina Press, 1979), 39.
15. For an interesting treatment see Charles Patrick Neimeyer, *America Goes to War: A Social History of the Continental Army* (New York: New York University Press, 1996).
16. Lawrence Delbert Cress, *Citizens in Arms: The Army and the Militia in American Society to the War of 1812* (Chapel Hill: University of North Carolina Press, 1982), 59.
17. "Washington's 'Sentiments on a Peace Establishment,'" in *The Draft and Its Enemies: A Documentary History*, edited by John O'Sullivan and Alan M. Meckler (Urbana: University of Chicago Press, 1974), 27–28.
18. "Knox Militia Plan, 1786," ibid., 36.
19. E. Wayne Carp, "The Problem of National Defense in the Early American Republic," in *The American Revolution: Its Character and Limits*, edited by Jack P. Greene (New York: New York University Press, 1987), 32.
20. Federalist 23, in *The Federalist Papers*, edited by Clinton Rossiter (New York: Mentor, 1961), 153.
21. Quoted in Charles A. Lofgren, "Compulsory Military Service under the

Constitution: The Original Understanding," *William and Mary Quarterly*, 3rd series, vol. 33, no. 1 (January 1976): 75.

22. David C. Williams, *The Mythic Meanings of the Second Amendment: Taming Political Violence in a Constitutional Republic* (New Haven: Yale University Press, 2003), 15–16. See also H. Richard Uviller and William G. Merkel, *The Militia and the Right to Arms, or, How the Second Amendment Fell Silent* (Durham, N.C.: Duke University Press, 2002).

CHAPTER EIGHT: CITIZEN SERVICE FOR THE AGE NOW UPON US

1. Drew Brown, "A Breaking Point for the Military?" *Philadelphia Inquirer*, January 26, 2006. See also Ann Scott.

2. For a good historical overview, see Barry M. Steniforth, *The American Home Guard: The State Militia in the Twentieth Century* (College Station: Texas A&M Press, 2002).

3. See James J. Carafano and John R. Brinkerhof, "Katrina's Forgotten Responders: State Defense Forces Play a Vital Role," Heritage Foundation Executive Memorandum #984, 5 Oct 2005.

4. The State Guard Association of the United States may be reached at: Box 1416, Fayetteville, GA 30214-1416. Phone: 770.460.1416, www.sgaus.org.

AFTERWORD

1. Tom Vanden Brook, "Army Exceeds Lowered Target for Recruiting through March," *USA Today*, April 11, 2006.

2. G2-forward.org, "Pentagon Still Years from Having Its Books in Order," April 7, 2006.

3. Jonathan Karp, "With New Rules, Weapons Projects Set Higher Costs," *Wall Street Journal*, April 10, 2006.

4. Oliver Poole, "Killings Lead to Brain Drain from Iraq," *Telegraph (UK)*, April 17, 2006. See also Sharon Behn, "Militias Force Thousands of Iraqis to Flee," *Washington Times*, April 19, 2006.

5. Associated Press, "Commanders Protest Policy That Lets Iraqi Troops Quit," *USA Today*, April 14, 2006.

6. Sarah Baxter, "US Plots 'Liberation of Baghdad,'" London *Sunday Times*, April 16, 2006.

7. William Matthews, "Study: U.S. Army Needs $25B over 2 Years for Damaged Gear," *Defense News*, April 25, 2006.

8. Mark Trahant, "Interest-ing Way to Look at Federal Debt," *Seattle Post-Intelligencer*, February 5, 2006.

9. Christopher Lee, "Pentagon Ends Bad-Work Bonuses," *Washington Post*, April 11, 2006.

10. Mark Mazzetti and Jim Rutenberg, "Pentagon Memo Aims to Counter Rumsfeld Critics," *New York Times*, April 16, 2006.

11. Fred Kaplan, "Could Rumsfeld Court-Martial the Retired Generals?" Slate.com, April 26, 2006.

12. Paul Kane, "A Peaceful Call to Arms," *New York Times*, April 20, 2006.

13. Paul Jelinek, "Draft Boards Stay Ready—Just in Case," Associated Press, April 20, 2006.

Index

About the Author

PHILIP GOLD is the author of five books, including *Take Back the Right*, along with more than eight hundred articles, columns, and reviews. He has served as a Marine officer, covered defense issues for a national news magazine, and was recently a Senior Fellow in National Security Affairs at the prestigious Discovery Institute in Washington, D.C. Gold holds a B.A. in history from Yale University and a Doctorate in history from Georgetown University, where he taught history and defense policy for fourteen years.

About the Type

The text of this book was set in Janson,

a misnamed typeface designed in about 1690 by

Nicholas Kis, a Hungarian in Amsterdam.

In 1919 the matrices became the property of the

Stempel Foundry in Frankfurt. It is an old-style

book face of excellent clarity and sharpness.

Janson serifs are concave and splayed;

the contrast between thick and thin storkes is marked.